Projects, Programs, and Portfolios in Strategic Organizational Transformation

Projects, Programs, and Portfolios in Strategic Organizational Transformation

James Jiang, Gary Klein, and Wayne Huang

BEP BUSINESS EXPERT PRESS

Projects, Programs, and Portfolios in Strategic Organizational Transformation

First published in 2020 by
Business Expert Press, LLC
222 East 46th Street, New York, NY 10017
www.businessexpertpress.com

ISBN-13: 978-1-94944-380-6 (paperback)
ISBN-13: 978-1-94944-381-3 (e-book)

Business Expert Press Portfolio and Project Management Collection

Collection ISSN: 2156-8189 (print)
Collection ISSN: 2156-8200 (electronic)

Cover and interior design by Exeter Premedia Services Private Ltd., Chennai, India

First edition: 2020

10 9 8 7 6 5 4 3 2 1

Printed in the United States of America.

Abstract

Projects are a part of everyday life in an organization. Tools and procedures for project management are well understood and applied. However, the management of projects by an organization for substantial transformation is less certain in both practice and study. An awareness of how to manage increasingly complex projects, and collections of projects, to achieve the benefits of organizational transformation becomes ever more crucial in the implementation of new strategies.

This book goes beyond a simple review of tools and techniques common in most publications of project management. We illustrate how the traditional practice of project management advances to handle the more complex problems inherent to strategic organizational transformation. The linkages among projects, operations, and the foundations of an organization provide a perspective of how an organization might pursue the difficult changes required of comprehensive transformation. The fashion in which the project world interacts with the executive world through successive layers of project management principles is prelude to operational benefits realization.

Keywords

strategy implementation; organizational transformation; project management; program management; project portfolio management; process integration

Contents

CHAPTER 1

Strategic Organizational Transformation

- Strategic organizational transformations respond to shifts in the environment to establish sustainable competitive capabilities.
- 70+ percent of corporations are expected to implement organizational transformations in the foreseeable future.
- Typically, only one-third of organizational transformations are successful, with diminished capacity or elimination as a result of failure.
- Strategic organizational transformations are a specific type of project suggesting the utilization of project management practices and techniques.

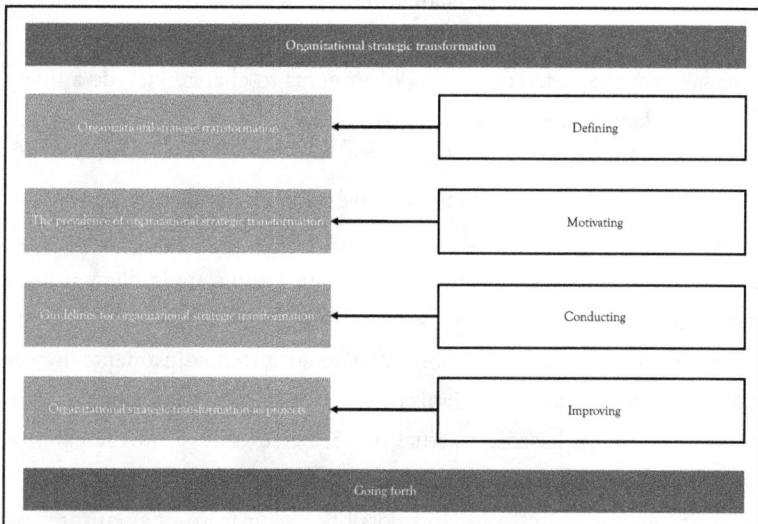

Chapter Structure

- Unlike traditional project management, transformation must continually focus on the management of multiple projects, environmental uncertainty, and organizational politics.

Strategic Organizational Transformation

Organizations make continual adjustments in response to changes in external factors and influences. Adjustments vary in degree according to requirements dictated not by the organization, but by the environment in which they operate. Product portfolios must adjust according to the changing demands of consumer markets. Adjustments might be a minor response to broaden options or make feature changes that satisfy an evolving preference of customers, such as a larger number of flavor choices for soft drink offerings or switching to recyclable packaging for storage and shipping. Changes due to transformation may be far more complex, such as entering new markets to counter the erosion in sales of outdated goods or moving into the market for entertainment content instead of relying on entertainment hardware. An organization must adjust to changes in the labor force as demands on talent shift to newer disciplines, leaving a shortage of skilled workers, especially in the fields of technology and analytics. Attracting and retaining desirable talent requires that organizations adjust to attitudinal changes regarding loyalty to both company and career. The examples could continue almost indefinitely, but suffice it to say that the different sources of impetus to change include a litany of market factors, regulations, investor requirements, societal pressures, and competitors.

When organizational change involves directional factors in response to or anticipation of environmental changes, such as vision, product positioning, or operational structure, then organizations are implementing a strategic transformation (Mintzberg and Westley 1992). Formally, strategic organizational transformation refers to advanced adjustments or core makeovers conducted by organizations to establish a sustainable competitive advantage based on actual or predicted changes in the external environment. Strategic transformation alters organizational capabilities, products, systemic processes, and possibly higher features as culture and leadership. In practice, environmental changes tend to occur more rapidly than essential transformations, resulting in a misalignment between the market and the organizational direction or a lag between strategic transformations and environmental changes. When a lag occurs, an organization is forced into more rapid, revolutionary strategic transformations (Johnson, Scholes, and Whittington 2005).

Organizations strive to maintain currency and relevance through continual improvements, each representing a small adjustment, but collectively transforming the organization and meeting both past and anticipated changes to the external environment and internal conditions. However, even an organization effective at continual improvement will someday be outstripped by the speed and magnitude of changes to their environment. Figure 1.1 illustrates how incremental change can be effective up to a point, but not beyond due to the emergence of large gaps.

At the start, an organization may effectively address the needs of their customers, investors, and employees through incremental changes instead of substantial transformation. As the environment changes, indicated by the line of change level, the organization proceeds with incremental steps to address change as indicated by the bars in Figure 1.1. For a time, the responses adequately address the changes to the environment as in Point A. At Point B, the speed of environmental change accelerates, leaving the ability of an organization to rise to the level of required changes through incremental transformations. At Point C, change continues in the

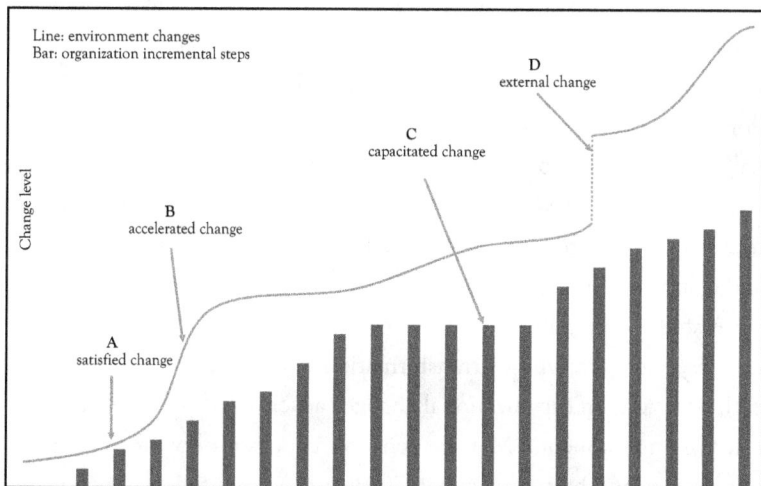

Figure 1.1 Incremental response to levels of change over time

environment, but the organization reached its capacity to change existing systems, practices, processes, or policies; perhaps the expense of marginal change exceeds the value, or technical limitations are reached. At Point D, a major shift in the environment occurs, perhaps due to technology, regulation, or social awareness. In Cases B, C, and D, the ability of an organization to make incremental change fails to maintain the required pace. Thus, there are times when an incremental approach is effective, and other times when a more revolutionary transformation is required.

Of course, the binary representation from incremental steps of transformation to larger revolutionary transformation is overly simplistic. The nature of incremental steps addresses long-term transformation typically associated with efficiency and profitability, while a revolutionary transformation results from challenging the beliefs of an organization. Incremental steps target adapting to smaller changes in the environment while continuing to rely on existing strengths and capabilities. Here, an organization accomplishes strategic transformation through a gradual process by making small-scale adjustments, slowly leading an organization from its current state to a future state while retaining strengths associated with operational capabilities and market advantages. Clearly, such an approach may maintain the stability of organizational operations while moving the organization to match the organizational transformation to environmental changes.

On the other hand, revolutionary transformation involves a substantial overhaul, perhaps requiring new capabilities, a new culture, and a new business model. In between incremental and revolutionary transformation lie many possibilities. Environmental change may require substantial operational improvements or product modifications, but no essential change to the business model or culture of the organization. Likewise, the reverse might also be true. Table 1.1 affords a comparative look at extreme and combined features.

A strategic organizational transformation is a tool for environmental response, and the type of transformation chosen depends uniquely on each situation, on organizational change capacity, and pressures from the external environments. Management must focus on how to implement transformations best to facilitate surviving and thriving. Implementing strategic transformation that is not well considered is not a way to

Table 1.1 Incremental versus revolutionary transformation

	Incremental	Combined	Revolutionary
	Gradual strategic transformation implemented over a long period	Gradual transformations punctuated with occasional radical transformations	Large-scale strategic transformation implemented over a short period
Time horizon	Long	Moderate	Short
Scope and scale	Small	Medium	Large
Planning basis	Anticipative	Reflective	Reactive
Resistance	Minor	Varied	Substantial
Focus	Opportunities	Opportunities and threats	Threats
Typical Impact	Operations	Business model	Almost everything
Intent	Adjust	Renovate	Overhaul

embrace change but more of a way to arrive at organizational extinction. Regardless of the location on the incremental to revolutionary scale, organizations must manage the transformation to achieve objectives of closing the gap with the environment. The transformation must be accomplished effectively and efficiently to leave the organization in the best competitive position possible.

The Prevalence of Strategic Organizational Transformation

Detailed data to characterize organizational effort are scarce due to differing perspectives on the threshold to be recognized as transformational change. Most researchers and authors use the term interchangeably, as transformation is a higher level of change involving more depth of impact for an organization. A 2016 study by the Corporate Executive Board (CEB, now a subsidiary of Gartner) asserts that organizations execute an average of five transformations over every three years. Of the firms considered, 78 percent indicated attempting deep transformations of culture or mission. Furthermore, 73 percent of corporations in the report estimate they will execute a major organizational transformation within the next three years. Only a small fraction expects to slow the pace of transformation.

Variety

Transformations arise from multiple reasons and in multiple contexts. Taking an organization from current status to a position aligned with the environment will involve any number of interest groups, require specialized knowledge from multiple disciplines, and necessitate management of change across a broad scope. The transformation will cross structural levels and structural divisions in an organization leading to a variety of perspectives. The CEO may view a specific initiative as a change to strategy, whereas a field sales representative may see only a change to the product portfolio. The manager of information technology may view a specific initiative through a narrow technology lens, whereas operations managers may view the same transformation as a change to the process.

Though organizations focus on moving the organization to meet strategic needs, determination of mission and strategy must supplant other initiatives in priority. Organizations must adjust to this primary aspect or face dire consequences. Corporations with decades of past success are not assured of survival in the current marketplace without adjusting to new realities. The number of longstanding corporate giants struggling in the market and with investor valuations continues to grow. Companies with novel vision and missions displaced many industrial giants not able to transform. Yet the tenure of new organizations is by no means assured if they cannot identify essential transformations and effectively manage required change. All remaining challenges of transformation pale in need to keep the mission and strategy of the organization in line with the environment. New strategies ignite the need for further transformation, either as a part of the same major transformation or as a series of anticipated minor changes.

The organizational structure must transform to place the talent in the best position possible to achieve strategic organizational goals. The effective organization of departments can provide channels to press the desired chain of command or autonomy. Altering responsibilities or roles of departments, teams, and people can improve responsiveness to clients in a transformation from a product push orientation to one of service pull. Mergers and acquisitions spark consideration of the best structure for the combined organization. Hiring, training, and retaining personnel for new roles and responsibilities becomes an essential element of transformation. Organizational structure may represent significant, rapid change with many stages in progress simultaneously, or with a more incremental approach to alignment.

Technology is often cited as a reason to transform an organization. This view is limiting, however. Organizations must align with the environment, not to technological advancement. No doubt, technology is powerful. The Internet of Things, advances in artificial intelligence, blockchain and secure contracts, and cloud computing enable further business opportunities in products and market or support more efficient means of operations, but these and other technologies are enablers of opportunity, not saviors of poorly designed strategy. Still, technology-driven transformation presents some of the most invasive change to the entire organization. Managing changes incorporating technology require extensive control and management to gain acceptance throughout the organization and achieve the expected benefits (Jiang, Klein, and Fernandez 2018).

As a product line ages, a transformation is essential. Product strategy is a clear example of how transformation in one area influences changes to others. An organization must determine whether to upgrade products, create new products, or attempt to reimage the existing product through marketing efforts. Any decision requires a certain level of change, impacts different responsibilities across departments, and could also be implemented as a major transformation or incremental changes often depending on the perceived urgency in meeting market demands. A focus on new product development may require installation of structural changes to bring development projects into an organization established on repetitive operations. Processes to produce new products affect operations. Departments may need to expand or retrench. Updating channels of distribution requires change. Structuring such a change process requires strong consideration of speed and scope.

As recent as a few decades ago, organizations began to recognize the critical need to manage organizational knowledge universally. Knowledge management practices and more effective management of intellectual capital drove the inclusion of new executives, systems, and processes. The same trend continues today with an emphasis on analytics, the art of turning extensive data into competitive advantages. Knowledge and analytics help an organization respond faster, make better decisions, and reveal new opportunities. An organization must be prepared to capitalize on knowledge advantages, sometimes requiring rapid changes of significant magnitude or simple adjustments to processes. Both the incorporation into the organization of knowledge practices and changes required to respond to revelations imply the need to properly manage change both incrementally and in rapid, large chunks.

At this point, we still have not described other contexts of transformation, such as changes to organizational culture, business tasks, and processes, or legal agreements and policy. However, a pattern is already established in the limited number of transformations described. The transformation may be rapid or paced, incremental or comprehensive, invasive or confined, and of broad or narrow scope. Transformations impact multiple layers of management, consider different time frames, and involve multiple skill categories. Regardless, one item of commonality is that transformations must be effectively managed to integrate all aspects of change seamlessly. Yet organizations are not typically structured or have the managerial capacity to transform continually.

Challenges

Currently, most strategic transformations fail to achieve the expected goals. The CEB report on more than 400 organizational transformations in various corporations worldwide found that only one-third of attempted transformations achieved desired levels of success, as shown in Figure 1.2. Failure of organizational transformations often results in major economic losses and corporate dilemmas: while it may be difficult to continue the transformation, abandoning transformation may cause dissatisfaction among stockholders or other

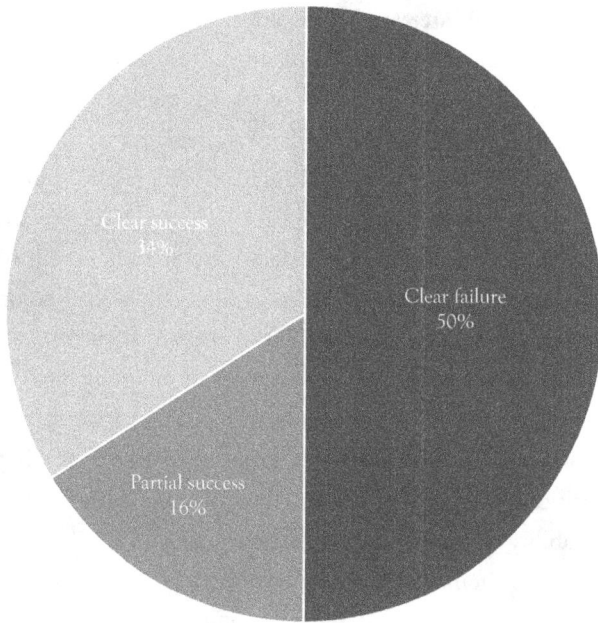

Figure 1.2 Success rates of strategic organizational transformations

stakeholders. Major failures in organizational transformation even result in corporate closure. Numerous challenges persist in successfully conducting a strategic transformation (Franken, Edwards, and Lambert 2009; Balogun, Hailey, and Gustafsson 2015). Challenges range across traits of the transformation, organization, stakeholders, and environment.

One primary challenge is the locus of power and resulting conflict. Power can be dispersed or centered in a particular body. Often, power is granted fully to ownership, resulting in short-term pressures to realize profitability and rapid growth. Major strategic shifts require excessive resources and place high risks on immediate and even continued financial rewards. In certain industries, unions may have undue influence, restricting how jobs may change or workforces may be reshaped. Change typically requires managerial autonomy and decentralization of authority to provide the flexibility and responsive essential for success. Organizations must often navigate the various streams of power while acting in ways contrary to powerful interests. The balance is often between risks due to change and risks due to a failure to change. This delicate balancing act often results in a combined approach to transformation.

Time poses a major challenge. Many strategic transformations push an urgent deadline. Transformation initiatives may require a long period to complete, fostering ownership worries about gaps in productivity. Initiatives forced by a crisis or extensive delay do not often permit sufficient time for analysis and planning. Success is more likely than failure when the need to change is determined well in advance to allow smoother transitions and windows for responding to dynamic environments. Pressures to meet predicted conditions or events, to be next to market, to counter competition, to return to profitability, to complete integration in mergers and acquisitions, to meet many other time-oriented constraints, can confound the ability to control the transformation.

Resource requirements can be overwhelming. An organization must commit funds, personnel, and time. If conducted during times of full operations, the additional requirements may be beyond the capacity of the organization. On the other hand, reducing operations will reduce the inflow of essential capital. Neither choice is pleasing, making it difficult to arrive at a satisfactory plan. Larger organizations may have the capacity to make incremental improvements on the way to a major transformation, but many organizations are forced into several simultaneously. Resources become scattered or scarce. Talent shortages appear as many changes require dedicated talent and new talent, indicating a lack of capability to complete a transformation. Managers cherish talent and are reluctant to relinquish control over limited resources once attained.

Further challenges stem from increased complexities of organizations. Transformations may cross multiple in-house functions, extend to regional facilities around the world, and even impact other organizations in a supply chain involved in the production of products and services. The spread of an organization involves a diversity of cultures, disciplines, and management levels. Therefore, when transformation occurs for any one strategy, the impacts are far-reaching and may involve multiple personnel, processes, structures, technologies, suppliers, and collaborators. This broad complexity makes strategic transformation plans far more complex and increases the risk of failure.

Scope of change addresses the breadth of reach for the change to implement. The scope also considers if big changes are required to culture, mission, or structure, or if shallow changes to processes and product offerings fit the bill. The broader the reach, the greater the control required, and the greater the risk of failure. The reverse side of scope also matters—retention. Core functions and competitive postures may go unchanged; these aspects may lie in unique departments and leave a number of people unaffected. Care must be taken to ensure that conflicts do not arise between those subjected to change and those protected from change.

An organization must be ready for the changes to be implemented. Strategic transformations begin with discussions and decisions among a few select individuals before the launch of any program of change. Yet the involvement of a large subset of the employees will prove essential before completion. Many will view change as unnecessary, merely a function of a bureaucratic whim. Participants must be properly motivated, which requires an understanding of the transformation purpose and process. Consideration of this factor, those aforementioned, and others that arise to each unique context, all require unique management skills and organizational structures to plan the strategic transformation and govern the process of change.

Guidelines for Strategic Organizational Transformation

There are numerous models that advise how organizations should initiate and implement strategic transformation. Searching the Internet and scouring academic journals, we located over 70 frameworks on how to complete a strategic transformation. Only a handful of sources mention project management techniques and those limit to a single perspective. They almost all have one commonality, a presentation of strategic transformation as having a sequential life cycle of inception to completion. Most focus on process, some consider behavior issues as the primary basis of transformation, and a few consider both aspects when striving to realize the changes necessary for transformation. Perhaps the most frequently described framework is credited to the famous psychologist Kurt Lewin, who considers the personal aspects of transformation and alludes

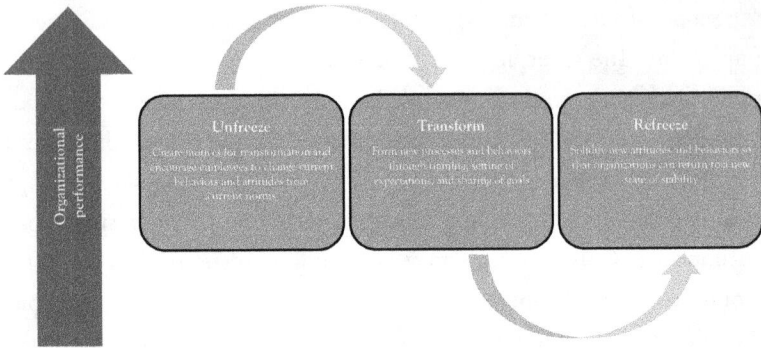

Figure 1.3 Lewin's model of transformational change

to actives that may complete the process (1997). The model is only the three phases shown in Figure 1.3. With a goal of improving performance, action must be taken to free current behavior and processes so that change may be conducted. Action taken during a change may temporarily lessen performance. Once personnel adjust to the new way of doing things, the new state should be made permanent (until the next major change).

The model is unique in that it clearly indicates an end has come to the old way of doing things. People must realize that they need to change, which often involves loss of ingrained processes, loss of relationships within the organization, and perhaps even loss of familiar surroundings. It is essential that people be motivated to make the required changes and surrender old habits. Negative feelings may be aroused during significant change, so a motivational jolt is critical. Moving into the phase of transformation requires inordinate effort about past expectations. The organization may suffer at the time, leading to uncertainty about the future for everyone involved in the transformation. Effort must be elevated to acquire new processes and skills. Burnout is a substantial risk along with discomfort due to visible degradation of organizational performance. Lastly, the organization enters a new state where norms, culture, and procedures represent a higher level of performance for the organization. Management must provide support to encourage the new state and reward those who adjust.

Models frequently mentioned by researchers include those of Kast and Rosenzweig (1973) and Schein (1965) described in Table 1.2. These models, and many others, focus on the steps of a transformative change. The model by Kotter (2009), also in Table 1.2, is similar to the process

Table 1.2 Strategic organizational transformation process models

Model	Steps
Kast and Rosenzweig's transformation process model	Review current status: review, reflect on, assess, and study internal and external organization environments
	Identify problems: identify existing problems and determine the need for organizational transformation
	Identify gaps: identify gaps between current and future states and analyze existing problems
	Design methods: propose and assess different methods for discussion and performance measurement and select appropriate methods
	Implement transformation: implement transformation according to chosen methods and action plans
	Review performance: assess and review results; if new issues arise, begin this process again from the start
Schein adaption cycle model	Assess internal and external environment changes
	Provide specific transformation information to relevant organizational units
	Change internal processes according to information provided
	Reduce or control the negative impacts of transformation
	Output new products and results generated after transformation
	Review and observe consistencies between internal and external environments to assess transformation results
Kotter transformation model	Generate a sense of urgency
	Establish a strong and stable transformation team
	Establish a vision and form strategy
	Communicate and promote transformation visions
	Authorize employees to implement actions to achieve visions
	Systemic planning and short-term benefits
	Implement organizational transformation
	Establish systems
	Culture formation

models, but adds a beginning step similar to unfreezing and a final step similar to refreezing. Based on these models and others presented in the many research papers, we find four key steps of strategic organizational transformation to be (1) assessment of current situations, (2) selection of new strategies, (3) implementation of strategic transformation, and (4) monitoring and review of strategic transformation.

Of these four key steps, assessment of current situations is the heart of strategic transformations, where organizational status and internal and external environments are analyzed to clarify the needs and motives of organizational transformation. This foundation is then used to design and plan a transformation strategy to guide strategic decisions. After confirming the direction and goals of the new strategy, the next step involves the implementation of strategy, which is key to the success of achieving strategic transformations. Therefore, it is necessary to continually monitor and review the implementation process to ensure timely and effective adjustments to strategy implementation.

However, the reliance on steps in a model is misleading. Organizations may have multiple transformations in progress that interact with each other and influence the internal environment evaluated. Monitoring must be continual. Environmental changes are not considerate enough to wait until transformation is complete, indicating that continual evaluation of the environment might interrupt a transformation initiative completely by making it moot, incorrect, or even escalate its importance. Organizations must develop managerial structures to be fluid and responsive, not related to a defined process.

Strategic Organizational Transformation as Projects

Concepts of project management are becoming more prevalent, and more managers are using project management techniques to implement strategic transformation (Partington 1996). Researchers view strategic transformation as a specific project or program in which well-established project management techniques apply (Caldwell 2003). Utilization of project management techniques can enhance success rates of strategic organizational transformations (McElroy 1996). Projects seem a natural structure for implementing strategic transformation. Projects address many of the difficulties described earlier, including the management of time, scope, budget, stakeholders, communication, and resources.

However, note that even though more scholars recommend and more managers apply project management techniques to implement strategic transformation, in actuality, managers often fail to understand or focus on the differences in strategic transformation projects to projects of less severity and complexity, and simply use traditional project management processes and techniques. Given the rates of success, such an approach is not as successful as desired. When viewing strategic transformations as projects, it is necessary to allow for the issues of complexity noted earlier. For our purpose, we deem differing complexities related to the following three factors:

1. *Complexities of strategic transformation projects stem from the fact that it is necessary to manage multiple projects (project combinations).* Implementation of new strategies at all levels within an organization is a task that must be accomplished through multiple projects rather than a single project. However, limited resources within an organization pose a basic difficulty in that multiple projects must be designed, timed, and completed in a network of interrelated projects. Additional complexities also arise during the conduct of the projects because limited resources must be effectively allocated and coordinated.

2. *Management complexities of strategic transformation projects stem from uncertainties in goals and solutions.* Traditional projects produce tangible products or relatively specific services. Project goals and procedures for most contexts are assumed to be well specified and clear for the duration of the project. However, strategic transformation projects are a type of "soft project," where outcomes may be intangible, and project goals are difficult to define at the initiation. Only as the transformation progresses do the goals crystallize and the means of achievement become evident. Even then, adjustments must be made to the goals and means as continued interaction with external environments reveals new directions. Therefore, there is uncertainty within strategic transformation projects at the start and throughout the life of the project. Traditional project management techniques cannot be used to manage dynamic projects where solutions and goals are both unclear to start, and evolving as the project progresses. Therefore, an inherent problem of strategic transformation projects is the management of uncertainty in project goals and solutions.

3. *Management complexities of strategic transformation projects arise from power and politics.* The very nature of strategic transformations is that

of a power struggle between potential and existing beneficiaries. In terms of strategic transformation projects, finding an effective compromise among organizational stakeholders is key to project success and often a game of politics. This factor may be addressed in the planning of traditional projects, but the dynamic nature of a transformation presents an ever-shifting landscape.

This book relies on research in project management and builds a framework for a strategic transformation from a project management perspective. Strategy development requires an understanding of the internal and external environments of the organization. An overview of the framework is in Figure 1.4, which shows the two halves of strategic transformation, strategy development, and strategy implementation. Typically, executives are the decision makers in the formulation of strategy. However, a statement of strategy is insufficient to move the organization forward. Thus, executives oversee the creation of strategic plans that then guide any organizational transformation. Lower management implements the plans to unfreeze, transform, and refreeze as required by the plans, normally with project management techniques organized as discussed in the remainder of this book.

The implementation side contains many temporary endeavors organized as projects. The core mission of each project is to generate and

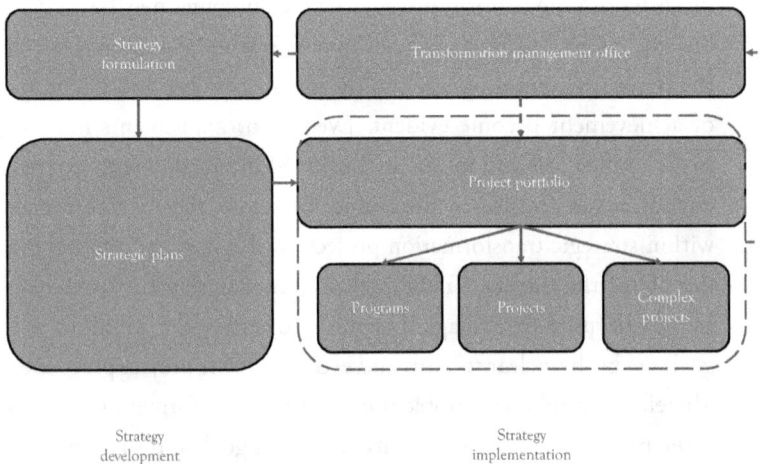

Figure 1.4 Strategy development and implementation in organizational transformation

produce outcomes under limited amounts of time, budget, and other resources while permanent structures (e.g., the executive team) work to ensure a strategic direction and pursuit of that strategic direction. A controlling entity, the transformation management office (or other permanent organizational control entity such as project management office, program management office, or change management office) obtains information on all projects within an organization and maintains consistency with strategy (Aubry, Hobbs, and Thuillier 2007). For example, project management offices organize information on project performance to provide a reference for the organization to adjust, remove, or add individual projects that reside in the collection of all projects.

The controlling office is a permanent structure that helps those in charge of the projects arrive at completion. The transformation management office further reports to the strategic decision makers. Those making the strategic decisions may then adjust organizational strategy according to organizational capabilities and any environmental shifts. These lines of direction appear in Figure 1.4. Strategic decisions direct planning, which in turn directs the management of installation actions organized as temporary projects, programs, and project portfolios. A responsible entity (the transformation management office) works with temporary entities (those in the dashed box in Figure 1.4) to gather feedback. The controlling office digests the feedback to suggest changes in implementation and inform executives for their future strategic formulations.

Going Forth

We examine the increasingly urgent strategic transformation challenges faced by organizations from a strategic organizational transformation perspective, developing a project management framework for planning and governance (decision makers and implementers), highlighting how effective project management can be used to manage strategic organizational transformation and ultimately enhance organizational performance.

The remainder of this book describes effective project management concepts for the implementation of strategic organizational transformation in terms of traditional project management, complex project management, program (multiple projects) management, project portfolio management, and conclude with a discussion of the organizational drivers of project management. Unlike other sources that focus solely on one type of project management when discussing strategic organizational transformation, we use a sequential approach in this book, proceeding from simple projects through comprehensive portfolios.

So that we may build understanding in increasing complexity, we apply a sequential structure in chapters 2, 3, 4, and 5. Chapter 2 starts with an introduction to traditional project management for temporary and one-time events within organizations. This type of project management is principally applied to strategic transformation projects where goals and solutions are clear. When there is the uncertainty of the solution methods, we apply complex project management as described in Chapter 3. Complex project management excels when facing structural complexities, technical complexities, and temporal complexities during the implementation of strategic organizational transformations. When uncertainty exists in project goals, when project deliverables are ambiguous, we switch to program management as described in Chapter 4 to respond to directional complexities of strategic organizational transformation. In Chapter 5, we also discuss project combination management for building portfolios. Traditional project management, complex project management, and program management focus on "how to conduct projects," but organizations are usually faced with the issue of "how to select projects" before project implementation. Determining the combinations of projects in a portfolio is a higher order function for an organization. The project combinations contain traditional projects, complex projects, and programs.

For each of chapters 2, 3, 4, and 5, we employ a standard configuration to best frame the appropriate project management techniques. Following a definition in each chapter, we consider, "Why do we need this type of project management?" (motive analysis). Following the motive is a definition of the type and relevant elements. Processes and specific techniques of each type of project management (processes) follow. Lastly, each chapter concludes with an exposition of project management boundaries and application limitations (limitations and challenges), which naturally leads to the subsequent chapters.

Beyond the project management considerations in chapters 2, 3, 4, and 5, we move on to organizational foundations in Chapter 6.

Organizational foundations include organizational transformation cultures, transformation structures, and transformation capabilities. Management of foundations enhances the strategic transformation ability of an organization in search of the best approaches to implement strategic transformation.

Discussion Questions

1. What complications arise from treating all environmental changes with incremental transformations?
2. What emotional factors or fears inhibit the implementation of transformation? What suggestions would you have for overcoming these inhibitions?
3. Can you think of a recent organizational transformation receiving wide coverage in the press? What impressions resulted in the market for that organization's product or service?
4. Governments often transform agencies or services due to societal changes. Identify a recent example. Can you identify any directive activity associated with unfreezing expectations or behaviors?
5. As a manager, how would you approach your subordinates about the need to make a major transformation?

References

Aubry, M., B. Hobbs, and D. Thuillier. May 2007. "A New Framework for Understanding Organizational Project Management through the PMO." *International Journal of Project Management* 25, no. 4, 328–236. doi: 10.1016/j.ijproman.2007.01.004

Balogun, J., V.H. Hailey, and S. Gustafsson. 2015. *Exploring Strategic Change*, 4th ed. Harlow, U.K : Pearson Education.

Caldwell, R. June 2003. "Models of Change Agency: A Fourfold Classification." *British Journal of Management* 14, no. 2, 131–142. doi: 10.1111/1467-8551.00270

CEB Inc (a subsidiary of). 2018. "Leading Successful Change." http://3mbang.com/p-1024545.html (accessed August 1, 2018).

Franken, A., C. Edwards, and R. Lambert. April 2009. "Executing Strategic Change: Understanding the Critical Management Elements That Lead to Success." *California Management Review,* 51, no. 3, 49–73. doi: 10.2307/41166493

Jiang, J., G. Klein, and W. Fernandez. January 2018. "From Project Management to Program Management: An Invitation to Investigate Programs Where IT Plays a Significant Role." *Journal of the Association for Information Systems* 19, no. 1, 40–57. doi: 10.17705/1jais.00480

Johnson, G., K. Scholes, and R.C. Whittington. 2005. *Exploring Corporate Strategy*. Harlow: Financial Times/Prentice Hall.

Kast, F.E., and J.E. Rosenzweig. 1973. *Contingency Views of Organization And Management*. Chicago, U.S: Science Research Associates.

Kotter, J.P. March-April 1995. "Leading Change: Why Transformation Efforts Fail." *Harvard Business Review* 73, no. 2, pp. 59–67.

Lewin, K. 1997. *Resolving Social Conflicts and Field Theory in Social Science*. Washington, DC, U.S: American Psychological Association.

McElroy, W. December 1996. "Implementing Strategic Change Through Projects." *International Journal of Project Management* 14, no. 6, 325–329. doi: 10.1016/0263-7863(95)00060-7

Mintzberg, H., and F. Westley. Winter 1992. "Cycles of Organizational Change." *Strategic Management Journal* 13, no. S2, 39–59. doi: 10.1002/smj.4250130905

Partington, D. February 1996. "The Project Management of Organizational Change." *International Journal of Project Management* 14, no. 1, 13–21. doi: 10.1016/0263-7863(95)00037-2

Schein, E.H. 1965. *Organizational Psychology*. Oxford, England: Prentice-Hall.

CHAPTER 2

Project Management

- When you observe the business world, and life itself, you find that projects are everywhere.
- The characteristics of project management include a clear goal and unambiguous output.
- Organizations constrain projects to schedule, budget, and product requirements (scope).
- Projects require balancing resources, relationships, and risks to achieve expected project goals and performance results.

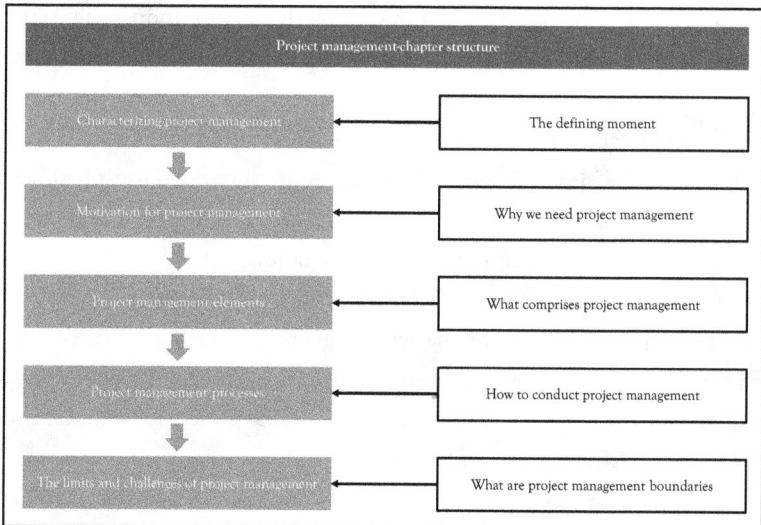

Project management-chapter structure	
Characterizing project management	The defining moment
Motivation for project management	Why we need project management
Project management elements	What comprises project management
Project management processes	How to conduct project management
The limits and challenges of project management	What are project management boundaries

Chapter Structure

Projects and Project Management

What's a Project?

Simply defined, a project is a temporary endeavor undertaken to create a unique product, service, or result (PMI 2017). Simplicity ends, however,

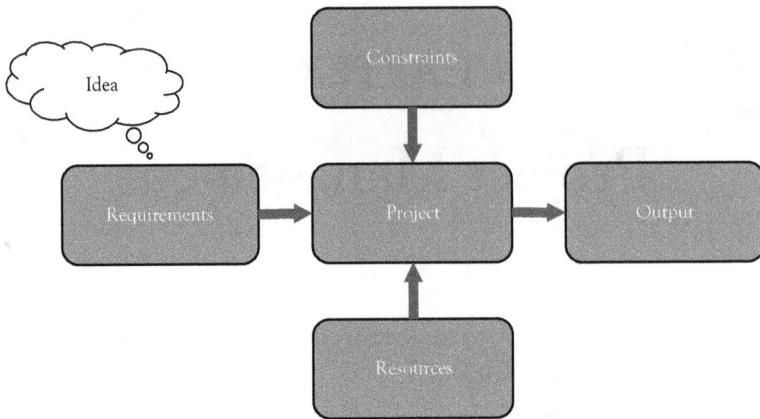

Figure 2.1 What makes a project a project?

with the definition. Consider the environment in which a project tran-spires, shown in Figure 2.1. An idea originates in the organization. It may involve any number of executives, managers, supervisors, or employees. If the idea survives initial analysis and debate, the organization codifies the idea as a set of requirements, setting the scope of the project. The require-ments could specify a new process for operating, a new or revised prod-uct for manufacturing, a facility to be constructed, or whatever else may encapsulate the idea. A project is initiated to produce the output that best meets the stated requirements. The project draws on the limited resources of the organization in competition or cooperation with other projects and continued operations. Internal constraints are set according to resource availability, the flexibility of the requirements, and criticality of timing. External constraints arise from competing and regulating interests within and outside the organization. Once complete, the project terminates, and the output passes to its intended operational life.

Projects come in a variety of contexts and types, each with unique features that often dictate the techniques employed during execution. Figure 2.2 shows a spectrum of project types, from those that have well-specified procedures to reach the desired output, to those that have more flexibility in how to arrive at the requirements. All projects have clear goals and specified requirements. An installation project might require the placement of new machinery in a manufacturing center. The project would involve major functions like the removal of old machinery,

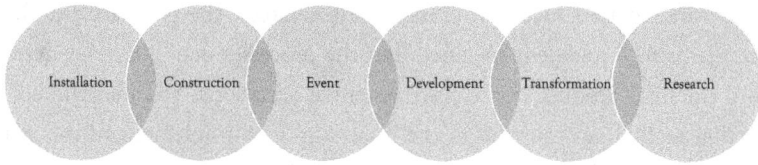

Figure 2.2 Spectrum of project types

the training of workers on the new equipment, the placement of the new machinery, testing of the equipment, and reinforcement of learning to reach production capacity. In this case, the goal may be to increase operating capacity 25 percent and the requirements precisely specified with the attainment procedures established.

A construction project might have a goal of building a new office center for the organization. The construction plan is set into the blueprints, and traditional construction processes applied. Specific designs provide adequate space and uniformity of appearance. Limited flexibility may exist in outsourcing certain steps or choosing the best equipment to build-out. An event may be for charity and set specific goals of publicity and fundraising, but allow flexibility in venue and activity. Development projects may be for new systems to meet information requirements. The goal may be to replace a legacy information system with one that is more streamlined or develop a new product for a particular market category. The goals can be very rigid, the information needs for the application quite specific, but the final product may evolve from the procedures employed. Replacing a legacy information system with one more integrated with other systems to reduce data errors and redundancy may have a very clear goal, but the system to be designed may be part of an agile system development with great flexibility to respond to the needs of the users.

A transformation project targets a change in the organization to better match operations to strategy (Söderlund 2010). From the proceeding chapter, a transformation project typically involves the incremental changes that are continually planned and executed. Substantial change requires more involved organizational management structures than a simple project, and those discussions follow in successive chapters. An incremental change that might be a single project would be adjusting employee behaviors by implementing new performance metrics. As an example, a call center may shift focus from evaluating employees on the number of calls handled to a focus on cross-sales generated. The goal is clear, the standards to implement specified, but the processes may not be evident, and the final product might have potential variations. Specific data collection techniques must be in the final output to implement in the call center, but the design of the collection technique will be one of the tasks to accomplish. Training is known from the start to be essential, but the actual conduct may not be in the requirements and must be tailored to best support the final output.

Research projects often have the goal of answering a specific question or solving a particular problem, but require latitude to explore many prospects and pursue a variety of solutions before arriving at any particular answer or result (Vom Brocke and Lippe, 2015). Of course, the delineation between the types is not sharp, and each type has the potential to become too complex for traditional project tools and methods. Further, since each project is unique, descriptive categories are effective at highlighting the difference between goals and output specifications, but not necessarily at leading one to the correct tools to succeed, where success at the level of projects is meeting the goals and requirements stated (scope) and staying within the constraints set by the organization on schedule and budget.

What's Project Management?

Project management is the application of knowledge, skills, tools, and methods to meet project requirements. This definition implies that an organization must effectively coordinate a large variety of resources to reach the specific goals of any project. Because project management requires a diverse knowledge of quantitative tools, estimation techniques, personnel behavior, and organizational context, project management has become a unique discipline filled by individuals with unique qualities who can advance a project to completion.

The discipline of project management is rooted in a long history of activity that seeks to develop a particular product under constraints of time and cost. The recognition of project management as a specific discipline and career goes back to the early 1950s in the construction industry, military weapons, and information technology projects. Less formally, project management has its roots in older construction projects such as the pyramids of Egypt, the aqueducts of ancient Rome, the castles and cathedrals in Europe, and the build-out of major infrastructure such as the Panama Canal. Project management tools and techniques enabled projects such as the Manhattan project, the Chunnel, and the Polaris submarine.

Over the years, certain standards of project management have come to include a distinct life cycle, management of cost, estimation of schedules, and a goal directed at a specific performance capability. Typical management duties of planning, motivating, directing, and controlling are required in managing a project to successful completion. However, the project manager does not carry the authority of typical line management, requiring additional abilities of leadership to motivate and coordinate across functional and organizational boundaries. Project managers often have no home within an organization. Yet project managers often hold the responsibilities for dealing with changes to the process, service, and products in modern organizations.

Understanding the tools and trade of the project manager is a critical objective of academic researchers and top management. Years of evolution in organizations and the results of academic research have led to a large body of knowledge about the required skills, attitudes, abilities, and tools essential to achieving successful completion of a project. Much of this understanding is incorporated into the standards set by professional societies dedicated to the project management professional. Guidelines for practice and behavior based on large bodies of historical information are captured in documents such as the Project Management Institute's body of knowledge publication (PMI 2017) and the International Project Management Association's competence baselines (Vukomanović et al. 2016). The growth in membership of professional societies for project management indicates the popularity of a project focus for many of the transformations in modern organizations.

The project manager, then, is responsible for taking the idea in Figure 2.1, determining the requirements that embody the idea, planning the activities of the project, adjusting for the available resources and constraints, to produce the deliverable best meeting the specified requirements. The idea originating the project can fall under any of the project types in the spectrum of Figure 2.2, but is generated before the inception of a project. As such, the quality of the idea itself is the responsibility of the executive choosing to pursue the idea, while the project manager is responsible for producing a deliverable to the specifications according to a specific schedule and budget. The severance of the idea from the process to deliver the idea delineates responsibility as well as rewards and credits for success. A poor idea can result in a successful project if the project manager can deliver the idea according to specifications, time, and budget. However, the poor idea will likely have no value to the organization. On the other hand, a great idea might be poorly managed during the project resulting in a product that is excessively late, way over budget, or a poor match to the specifications. Success requires that the executives choosing the projects properly execute their responsibilities, and that the project manager competently arrives at a project completion meeting expectations.

In the transition arena, a simple project might be based on an executive decision to reform the sales team from a single point of contact philosophy to a pooled service group philosophy. The project might require reshuffling personnel according to talent, background knowledge, regional affiliation, or another appropriate determinant. A time frame and

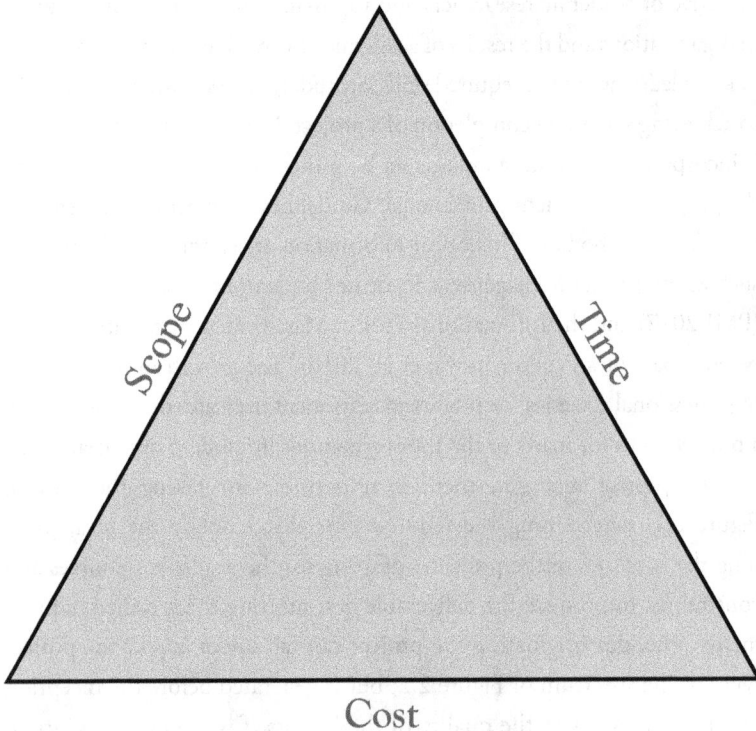

Figure 2.3 *The iron triangle of project management*

budget would be established for completion. Specific objectives would be established to, perhaps, guide the reallocation of personnel in terms of improving service to the client base or expansion of the market. Modifications to existing business processes may also be required. Potential trade-offs among the specifications or scope, the time to completion, and the cost of achieving the deliverable represent a maxim known as the iron triangle in projects. This triangle is represented in Figure 2.3. As in most any management situation, delivery to a fixed level of requirements can be adjusted to a shorter schedule with increased costs or similarly maintain lower costs through schedule slippage. Likewise, cost or schedule may be reduced by reducing the scope of the requirements.

Of course, while planning a project, the project manager must consider many externalities in the determination of requirements, cost, and time. These are represented in Figure 2.1 as the constraints and resources that impact the project in achieving the deliverable. These externalities run a large gamut that includes issues of human resource management, procurement, risk management, and communication with a variety of stakeholders. All of these are within the boundary of the project to be managed and combined to produce the final deliverable. This grouping

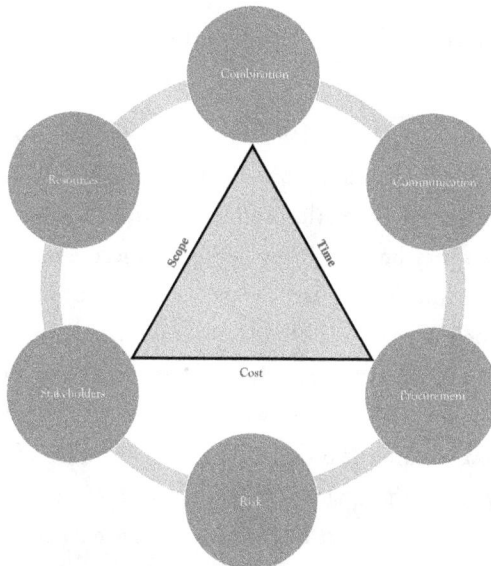

Figure 2.4 Project management boundary

is represented in Figure 2.4. Consideration of all activities within these boundaries is the scope of work required of the project manager.

Project Management Motives

The activities of accomplishment in business include "operational activities" and "project activities." Of these, operational activities are those that must be repeated and continually performed to maintain the daily functions of a business. Project activities are nonroutine tasks that businesses perform to achieve specific objectives (the deliverable). The biggest difference between a project and operational activities is that project activities tend to be temporary and one-time activities (Turner and Müller 2003). These characteristics indicate that project activities have a limited amount of time and budget dissimilar from the regular concept of production schedules and productivity. If businesses apply traditional management concepts used for operational activities to project activities, they will find it difficult to provide quality products and services according to time and cost constraints. Even if the deliverable matches the specifications, businesses may fail to achieve expectations of cost and schedule (Atkinson 1999).

Project Management Can Create Unique Products, Services, and Results

Operational activities tend to follow repetitive organizational processes. Conversely, because projects are unique, there may be elements of uncertainty and difference between the products, services, and results produced. Project activities may be completely new for project team members, with more detailed planning required compared with routine work. Projects can be developed at any level of an organization, involve one person or many people, and encompass only one organizational unit, multiple units, or even multiple organizations.

Projects develop unique products, services, or results while managing costs, delivery time, and quality. Project deliverables may be tangible or intangible. Even though there might be repetitive elements in the results and activities of certain projects, this repetitiveness does not affect the core uniqueness of projects. For example, in construction projects, the same or similar materials are utilized by the different projects, but each one is unique due to differences in location, design, environment, circumstance, and stakeholders.

Projects can generate:

- A product that may be a component of another product, an upgraded version of another product, or a finished product;
- A type of service or the capability to provide a certain service (e.g., support capabilities for production or logistics);
- An improvement over existing product lines or service lines (e.g., implementation of six sigma to reduce defect rates);
- Performance results, for example, in the form of knowledge or files (e.g., knowledge generated from research projects which can be used to determine the existence of certain trends or whether new processes are beneficial to society).

With Project Management, There Is Strong Cost Management

The amount of resources that can be deployed and utilized for a project is typically limited. To control costs for a business, project managers have to consider and plan total budgets for a project. In other words, the project budget is one of the keys to start a project. Overly high or unreasonable project budgets can cause project sponsors to abandon projects. Therefore, it is necessary to budget and set costs before starting any project. Without a reasonable plan for cost management, it is difficult to ensure that projects do not exceed their budgets; once a project exceeds its budget, this can signify failure.

With Good Project Management, Results Are Achieved On Time

Often, the time of project completion is set by the environment. A transformation to pursue new markets must be completed before competitors can capitalize on delays. New products may have seasonal demands, and a delay might mean the market cannot be breached for an extra year. If a project is not completed within the given amount of time, this signifies the failure of said project. Therefore, it is necessary to systemically plan projects from start to finish plotting the actions of the project to a timed commitment. Completion dates are viewed as hard commitments by those expecting results. Thus, in conjunction with budgets, planned schedules and techniques to control actions to plans becomes an important activity.

With Project Management, There Is Strong Quality Assurance

Within a project, the term "quality" refers to the fulfillment of client expectations and demands—meeting the requirements with the deliverables. In the long run, clients mainly remember the quality of results. Dissatisfaction stemming from an output that fails to pass muster endures much longer than the satisfaction derived from a project that is completed on time and under budget. Systemic project management is the best way to ensure routine quality control over the deliverable. Project management makes it possible to identify and correct problems promptly, which reduces losses and delays caused by redoing erroneous work, and wards off project failures. The key point is that without project management, it is highly difficult to find a balance between cost, quality, and delivery time. When planning project budgets, it is necessary to balance project resources and delivery time, and also ensure that project results meet expected goals. Project managers, therefore, need to find a reasonable sweet spot between project budgets and delivery time; this sweet spot is the "quality" of the project.

The Deliverables of Project Management Have a Far-Reaching Impact

Even though participation in and duration of projects tend to be temporary and a one-time sequence of activities, this does not indicate the products, services, or other results of a project are temporary. Projects typically generate permanent results. The social, economic, and environmental impacts of a project usually last much longer than the project itself. For example, a project for the construction of a national monument creates an output that can endure for centuries (Edum-Fotwe and McCaffer 2000).

In summary, project management on the one hand balances costs, delivery time, scope, and quality, and on the other hand differs from operational activities in that project activities can generate unique products, services, and results with a long-lasting impact. Therefore, management techniques of project activities are widely used in business circles.

Elements of Project Management

Within the boundary of a project lie elements that categorize the activities involved. The elements represent major categories of activity that fall within the purview of the project manager. Management of the project boundary ensures that projects execute only the work required for the deliverable. The boundary is quite porous; however, as a constant interchange with other units in the organization is essential to conduct the activities within the individual elements. The purpose of this book is not to provide detailed information on project management elements, but to highlight the issues that arise. To that end, we give brief descriptions of the elements involved in managing the project boundary. Greater information is available in sources such as the Project Management Body of Knowledge of the Project Management Institute (PMI 2017).

Project Time Management

Project time management ensures that all required project processes complete on time. Time management requires a plan, presented as a schedule, and methods to monitor progress against the schedule. The schedule itself describes the work that is to be accomplished over time.

Scheduling is one of the basic requirements of project planning, yet the estimation process is one of the more complex tasks. The first step in completing a schedule is usually the development of what's known as a work breakdown structure. The work breakdown structure segments the project into smaller packages, known as work packages, that can be sequenced into a schedule. Each work package is an identifiable segment of the tasks required to complete the project. A work package should be an independent unit that allows an accurate estimate of the time for completion and associated costs.

Work packages are then sequenced on a calendar that indicates the order in which they are to be completed based upon the precedence requirements of one work package to the next. When all work packages have been placed on the schedule, the schedule permits a projection of the total time of completion for the project, scheduling of resources, and an estimation of overall costs mapped to the calendar.

With the schedule complete, the project manager can maintain control over time by comparing the actual status of the tasks completed to the plan. Variances in progress to the schedule will require adjustments either to the plan or to the dedication of resources to specific activities. The planned schedule is, thus, a critical tool for determining aspects of time and cost.

The ability to break a large project into smaller independent units, such as the work packages, is a critical skill in the management of time. Estimating the times to complete the work package can be a difficult and tedious process on its own. However, when sufficiently detailed and isolated, the work packages make the estimation process feasible and more reliable. Conceptually the process described takes a project of any magnitude and breaks it down into smaller, manageable segments.

Project Cost Management

Project cost management ensures that projects complete within the approved budget by managing all processes relating to the planning, estimation, budgeting, financing, fundraising, and control of costs. Managing costs goes hand-in-hand with the management of time. The same work packages that enable an accurate estimation of time also enable an accurate estimation of direct costs through segmentation. Just as the overall time to complete a project is estimated by accumulating the times of the work packages, the overall direct cost is determined by accumulating the individual work packages. The direct costs might include materials, labor, equipment rental, and identifiable support. Overhead and administration are attached to the individual work packages based upon the needs of the organization, perhaps allocated as a percentage of time or labor or another mechanism that the organization deems appropriate. Once complete, controlling cost is done by tracking expenditures and comparing them with the planned budget at any point during the project. As with variances in time, a significant variance from the budgeted to actual expenses must be addressed.

Project Quality (Requirements) Management

Project quality management encompasses the implementation of existing processes and activities relating to organizational quality policies, goals, and responsibilities, ensuring that projects fulfill expected requirements. Thus, quality management involves assuring that the requirements as specified are met, satisfying the scope of the deliverable. Within project environments, quality management often utilizes policies and programs of the organization and executes quality assurance systems in place. Typically, quality management involves developing a plan, assuring quality is met, and implementing a quality control program. Quality planning identifies the standards to which the project will be held, both for the specifications of the deliverable as well as standards the organization holds important such as ISO certification. Quality assurance is typically set by performance criteria to which the project will be held. Quality control is then checking for variance in the work results against the standards set during planning. Again, variances require adjustments. It becomes critical to ensure quality continuously during a project, since the earlier variances are captured, the lower the cost of correction.

Project Resource Management

Project resource management encompasses the full range of resources, including personnel, equipment, supplies, raw materials, and facilities. As with time and costs, resources are typically allocated to individual work packages, which allow the precise determination as to when a resource will be required for the project. However, projects must compete with operations and other ongoing projects for the limited resources within an organization. Looking at the human resource aspect, project teams are composed of personnel who take on different roles and responsibilities to complete projects. Project team members may have different skills, may work full time or part-time, and may be working on more than one project at any particular time. Thus, resource management is not just the assignment of a resource to a particular work package and then assuming availability when required, the project manager must work with other departments and projects within the organization to assure the availability of required talent when needed. The same concerns arise for specialty equipment and facilities during a project. The lack of availability of the resource, whether personnel or physical, will necessarily delay the project, extending the time of completion or adding to costs.

Project Communication Management

Project communication management encompasses all processes relating to project information, such as timely planning, collection, generation, delivery, storage, indexing, management, control, monitoring, processing, and presentation to essential recipients. Project managers spend much, if not most, of their time on communicating with team members to control the progress of the project and stakeholders external to the project to inform of progress and remain informed of possible influences arising outside the boundaries of the project. External stakeholders may be from within the organization (at all levels of an organization) or from outside the organization. Effective communication builds a bridge between project stakeholders, connects stakeholders with different organizational backgrounds, levels of expertise, viewpoints, and interests. Making certain each stakeholder receives necessary information in a timely fashion is critical for maintaining progress as well as a favorable political atmosphere.

Project Risk Management

Project risk management encompasses processes relating to the identification of risk, analysis of risk, and control of risk. The goal of risk management is to increase rates and impacts of positive events on a project, and to decrease the rates and impacts of negative events. The identification of risks is the first step in enabling prevention of delays or extra costs. Various approaches to identify risks exist in practice. Project managers can consider information from previous projects, refer to predefined checklists for project risk areas such as technology, consider issues in personnel records that indicate missing skills and training, refer to results of audits on project management capability, or rely on reviews conducted by peers and senior management. Once identified, risk should be quantified in terms of their likelihood of occurrence and the damage due to the particular risk. Risks of low probability and low impact are typically ignored, while others are considered more severe. Those risks considered more severe in terms of either consequence or probability should be addressed during planning. The plan should specify how potentially damaging an identified risk can be, and when it may surface during the project. The plan should also consider techniques to mitigate the damage specific risk might create to the completion time or cost of the project. Mitigation techniques might involve using alternate technologies than originally planned, nonstandard operating procedures to avoid historical problems, or require additional talent be hired to fill gaps or prepare for exigencies. Those risks that remain unmitigated should have contingency plans to avoid delays created during a project by having courses of action already determined rather than forcing crisis management.

Project Procurement Management

Project procurement management relates to the obtainment of required resources. The determination of essential resources is established during the planning of a project. Resources available within the organization must be arranged through the structure provided by the organization. Since resources are shared by many projects and even operations, procurement often involves negotiation with other departments, projects, and even executives. Agreements are documented and guaranteed through charter arrangements within the organization. When resources from outside the organization are required, procurement involves contracting for services and supplies. For larger projects, the nature and structure of contracts are fundamental to the success of the project. Performance warranties are mandatory to prevent damage to the project by nondelivery of a contract's agent. The presence of external contracts also requires the inclusion of contract administration in the work packages of the project.

Project Stakeholder Management

Project stakeholder management encompasses the processes needed for the following tasks: identification of all personnel, groups, or organizations that may impact on or be impacted by the project; analysis of stakeholder expectations of and their impacts on the project; and establishment of appropriate management strategies to effectively deploy stakeholder participation in project decision making and implementation. Stakeholder management also includes continued communication with stakeholders to understand stakeholder requirements and expectations, facilitate problem solving, manage conflicts of interest, and secure stakeholder participation. Importantly, the project manager must understand the impact that supportive, indifferent, and hostile stakeholders might have on the final deliverable.

Combination of Project Management Elements

Every project includes the aforementioned elements to one degree or another. Each of the elements is a piece of the project management puzzle. The project manager must combine all of the activities carried out by the project management team. Even though the project management elements tend to be well defined and mutually independent, they may in practice overlap or interact in ways that are beyond the scope of published guidelines and incorporated into the process of managing a complete, successful project.

The Project Management Process

Apart from categorizing the elements involved in project processes, it is important to structure a sequence for completion of a typical project. This requirement fits well with the conceptual representation of a project life cycle. For the life cycle, there is a specific beginning, a recognizable set of activities, and a conclusion to every project. This suits the nature of projects as one-time structures to realize a very specific deliverable. Figure 2.5 shows a generic life cycle for most project types. An idea initiates the project; a plan is developed to meet the requirements that embody the idea;

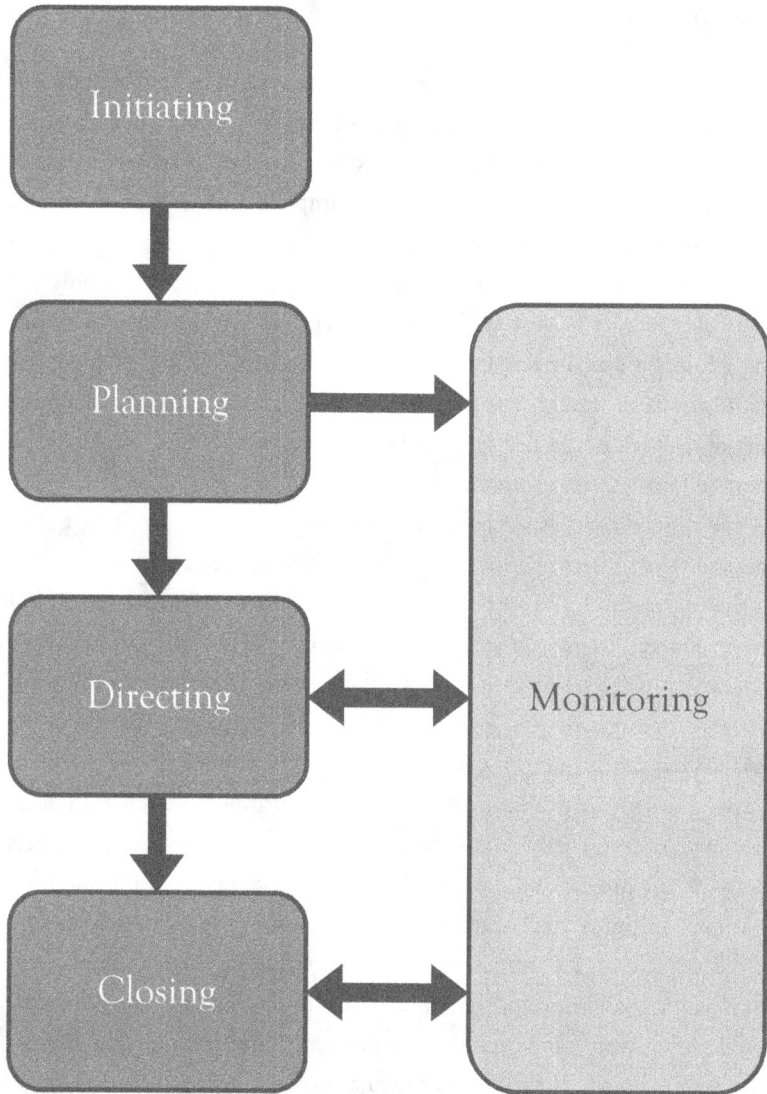

Figure 2.5 Life cycle of a project

and the project manager directs the project to closure with the given specifications, resources, and constraints. (The strict flow from one process to the next may be altered upon the reevaluation of a project or the choice of iterative methodologies such as agile project management.) Additional control procedures monitor the progress for necessary adjustments.

Initiation Process

The main purpose of initiation processes is to ensure that all preparation work is fully completed before project inception and that all stakeholders are fully committed. The processes begin once executives, or other authorities, decide to launch a project to implement the idea as a formal initiative for the organization. It is during the initiation that the organization must encapsulate the idea to proceed to a project. Not only are the goals for the project established and codified during initiation, but the project is synchronized with the operations and policies of the organization. Even though the project runs with a good deal of autonomy, the organization still has set policies and traditional roles that must be honored for a project to proceed.

For this reason, it is important to define the relationships that exist between the project and the remainder of the organization. For example, if the organization has specific practices for quality control, those should be considered important structures to incorporate into the project. Specific roles in the organization define the relationships between the project and the organization. For example, if a project management office is established as the governing authority for projects, then the project must have its ties to the project management office firmly established. Integration with the organization is established through a hierarchy of contracts between the project and the organization that establishes responsibilities, outputs, and governance structures fully defining the boundaries of the project. For example, certain organizations might require simple charters that define these relationships while others might have a formal proposal process that would indicate how the project is governed. Always imperative is a statement of the project's requirements.

In addition to establishing how the project fits into the organization as a whole, relational aspects of the project are also determined at this time. The organization appoints a formal sponsor or champion. The organization appoints a project manager. The goals or objectives are codified as a formal statement of output. Parameters on budget and completion time are established. The main activities of initiation processes include generation of the project authorization documents, confirmation of stakeholders, establishment of project management teams, defining the

Table 2.1 Processes and elements of project management

Elements	Project management processes				
	Initiating	Planning	Directing	Closing	Monitoring
Time management		✓	✓		✓
Cost management		✓	✓		✓
Quality management		✓	✓	✓	✓
Resource management		✓	✓		✓
Communication management		✓	✓	✓	✓
Risk management		✓	✓	✓	✓
Procurement management		✓	✓		✓
Stakeholder management	✓	✓	✓	✓	✓
Combination	✓	✓		✓	

relationship between the organization and the project, assigning governance and monitoring responsibilities, and project initiation meetings with active stakeholders. Initiation tasks are conducted by governing members of the organization, the project sponsors, the project manager, and key members of the project team. Project sponsors and project committees, such as a steering committee or project management office, provide guidance and progress reviews.

This early in the life cycle of a project, only a few of the elements previously described are activated. In particular, stakeholder management is critical. Building relationships with and developing an understanding of the executives and sponsors is best done early. Other actors in the organization impacted by the output of the project should be identified at this stage and prepared to take their role in later stages. A high level of the combination element is critical. Even though we defer details of schedule and cost and quality to the later stages, the organization does have guidance concerning overall cost and completion time to gain advantage from the expected output. All these aspects must be considered simultaneously with an overall perspective, nothing in isolation. Table 2.1 highlights this overlap of elements and processes within the initiating stage, as well as the overlap for remaining elements and processes in later stages.

Planning Process

The purpose of planning is to ensure that all tasks are identified and scheduled to produce the promised deliverable. Planning begins by considering the output of the initiating stage. This is typical of a staged project plan where the output from one stage is the input to the subsequent stage. Thus, planning takes all of the organizational preparation and establishes a blueprint to arrive at the required output. Table 2.1 indicates that every element of project management is involved in the planning stage. An understanding of each element is required to develop the plan and allow for the monitoring of progress. For example, the project manager is responsible for developing a schedule that is used to control the progress of the project. Quality practices are established that are commensurate with those of the organization's expectations for the output as well as the standards of practice the organization follows. In short, a plan describes project goals, risks, quality, resources, delivery time, budget, communication, procurement, and how the progress is monitored.

The relationship between the key players of the project team is further developed in this stage. An organization should establish a rewards program for the project team members. The rewards must encourage productive work. The project manager establishes behavioral expectations for the team and provides training as necessary to conduct activities of the project. Communication channels, contribution contracts, expectations of response time, and clear assignment of responsibilities all lead to a productive atmosphere for the project team. The project team must prepare for conflict among themselves as well as external stakeholders.

Defined procedures to resolve conflicts are essential in maintaining continual progress.

An early step in planning is to choose the project management methodology, such as whether one will pursue a waterfall approach or an agile approach in the development of an information system. The project management methodology influences the elements. For example, work packages defined in the work breakdown structure differ depending upon the methodology chosen. As the segments defined by work packages change, schedules, costs, responsibilities, resources, and stakeholder management will all change.

Planning tasks are typically the responsibility of project managers and the project management team. It is during the planning stage when many of the traditional project management tools come into play. Gantt charts illustrate scheduling. Communication plans dictate the timing and content required to inform stakeholders of progress. Risk analysis highlights areas of concern to include indicators, mitigation, and contingencies. Ample commercial software and quality shareware exist to support the decision making of planning and document the output of the planning stage for use in successive stages.

Directing Process

The intense activity of completing the deliverable defines the directing processes, when the project manager directs the application of resources, assigns the division of labor, and controls the quality of project progress toward the final product. The plans from the prior stage provide the blueprint required to take the specifications of the project's goal to completion with the deliverable that matches best the specifications. Project team members assume the roles defined and take the actions required. At all times, the project manager is concerned with every element in directing the team to the final product. Many of the same tools used in the planning stage will transit to the directing stage. The schedules built, the budgets made, the communication plans formed, and all of the other planning tools and documents assist the project manager and project team in successfully delivering the final product.

Closing Process

The closing processes represent the termination of the project. At this time, the product is complete. Though governance activities helped direct the project to successful completion, this handoff to other stakeholders can be problematic. If those who benefit from the product of the project are not properly prepared, then even the most successful project might not deliver a benefit to the organization. It is for this reason that stakeholders were involved in all the earlier phases to assure value will be realized.

The project team extracts value from an assessment of performance. Which processes in earlier stages were effective? How effective were the communication channels at keeping stakeholders informed? What organizational structures helped or hindered the progress of the project? Any lesson learned should be documented and placed in a knowledge base maintained by the organization. Any variance in completion to the original plans should be researched to determine cause and recorded as a possible risk to future projects. These tasks are conducted by project managers and project team members to capture knowledge for the organization.

Monitoring Process

The main purpose of monitoring processes is to ensure that all progress and problems of a project are effectively investigated, recorded, analyzed, assessed, reviewed, and processed. Monitoring is a critical feature of project governance and is established at the inception with details determined in the planning stage. Monitoring requires that a baseline be set for all features measurable, such as schedule, budget, and quality. The controls of monitoring may be frequently applied and spaced periodically. When indicators show a variance, the variance must be reconciled or corrected. It is possible that the correction might involve a rescheduling, conducting additional tasks, a redesign of the output, or even potential termination of the project.

As shown in Figure 2.5, monitoring processes sit over the three later stages of the project life cycle. The planning stage provides the baseline against which project progress is monitored and is a precursor to any monitoring activity. The controls placed in the directing and closing stages feed information to the monitoring processes for evaluation. The monitoring itself might lead to justifying actions of direction and closure through the feedback of information. The tasks related to project control are mainly conducted by project managers and project team members. However, responsibility for determining action based on feedback from the controls will vary by organizational structure and may include a project management office and sponsor.

Limitations of Traditional Project Management

Project management is a valuable productivity tool for organizations and appropriate for many contexts and applications. However, the improper application of project management to complex or uncertain goals can be disastrous. Advances in Internet and communication technology impact the speed of change for an organization, making projects of long duration problematic. Complexities lead to situations where management and control requirements exceed the capabilities of standard practices. Perhaps the biggest challenge comes from the fact that project managers are now faced with ever-greater uncertainty. These uncertainties include market uncertainties, organizational uncertainties, and even uncertainties brought about by obscurities of project goals and results. The question of how to manage projects with high uncertainty is a challenge faced by traditional project management. Other patterns have emerged over several decades that require an expanded view of how to deliver outputs in an environment requiring continual transformation to meet accelerating changes. For example, these patterns include:

- Advances in information technology and increased prevalence of outsourcing tighten the connections between businesses requiring a response by transforming supply chains and fulfillment strategies.

- Charles Handy (2001) wrote that business models would undergo great changes, and that future businesses would fall into one of two categories: "elephants" and "fleas." Elephant businesses are those composed of different enterprises that form strategic alliances. Flea businesses connect independent workers as unique organizations in their own right. Organizational structures must transform to relate to the new environment.

Many environmental trends require some degree of transformation by an organization. The speed, magnitude, and complexity of the required transformation may be beyond the capacity of traditional project management. Changes to the market, competitors, and business partners of an organization are often unpredictable, with the subsequent uncertainty also proving problematic. Projects emerged as a productive way to produce a well-defined output and not an output that is ambiguous, uncertain, and even unimagined. As organizations must transform to meet greater uncertainty and complexity, we must expand the traditional approach to project management.

Discussion Questions

1. Do your colleagues understand the difference between operations and projects? If not, how would you explain the difference using examples from your organization?
2. What lines of communication must be opened between project managers and executives in an organization? What information do you believe should be exchanged?
3. How does the concept of schedule change across the different project types in Figure 2.2?
4. If the driving force behind a project is a well-defined deliverable, how can projects develop new products or services?
5. Managing a project informs future projects. How might you ensure that the lessons learned reach across project boundaries?

References

Atkinson, R. 1999. "Project Management: Cost, Time and Quality, Two Best Guesses and a Phenomenon, Its Time to Accept Other Success Criteria." *International Journal of Project Management* 17, no. 6, 337–342. doi: 10.1016/S0263-7863(98)00069-6

Edum-Fotwe, F.T., and R. McCaffrey. 2000. "Developing Project Management Competency: Perspectives from the Construction Industry." *International Journal of Project Management* 18, no. 2, pp. 111–124. doi: 10.1016/S0263-7863(98)90075-8

Handy, C. 2001. "Tocqueville Revisited: The Meaning of American Prosperity." *Harvard Business Review* 79, no. 1, pp. 57–63.

PMI Standard Committee. 2017. *PMBOK® Guide*, 6th ed. Newton Square, PMI.

Söderlund, J. 2010. "Knowledge Entrainment and Project Management: The Case of Large-Scale Transformation Projects." *International Journal of Project Management* 28, no. 2, 130–141. doi: 10.1016/j.ijproman.2009.11.010

Turner, J.R., and R. Müller. 2003. "On the Nature of the Project as a Temporary Organization." *International Journal of Project Management* 21, no. 1, 1–8. doi: 10.1016/S0263-7863(02)00020-0

Vom Brocke, J., and S. Lippe. 2015. "Managing Collaborative Research Projects: A synthesis of Project Management Literature and Directives for Future Research." *International Journal of Project Management* 33, no. 5: 1022–1039. doi: 10.1016/j.ijproman.2015.02.001

Vukomanović, M., M. Young, and S. Huynink. 2016. "IPMA ICB 4.0—A Global Standard for Project, Programme, and Portfolio Management Competences." *International Journal of Project Management* 34, no. 8, 1703–1705. doi: 10.1016/j.ijproman.2016.09.011

CHAPTER 3

Complex Project Management

- Complex project management targets well-defined objectives but lacks clarity in the means of achievement.
- We may naively believe that clients articulate their actual needs, but when we discover the truth, we realize there's a problem, and that's when everything becomes complicated.
- Complexity arises from sources of organizational structure, advancing technology, the evolution of markets and the environment, and the ambiguity of project goals and direction.
- Complex project management abilities are limited most by the ambiguity of goals and direction.

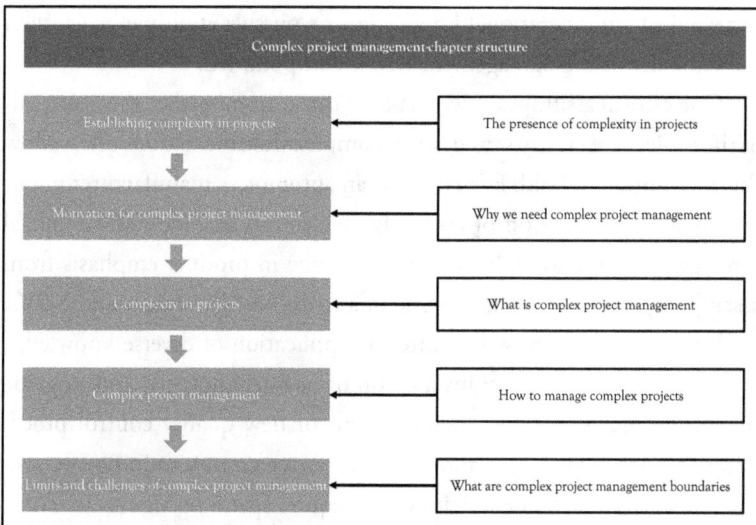

Complex project management-chapter structure

Establishing complexity in projects	The presence of complexity in projects
Motivation for complex project management	Why we need complex project management
Complexity in projects	What is complex project management
Complex project management	How to manage complex projects
Limits and challenges of complex project management	What are complex project management boundaries

Chapter Structure

Complex Project Management

Techniques for the management of projects are well established and doc-umented. An organization typically has a portfolio of tools and expe-rienced project managers to lead to the successful conclusion of the traditional projects described in the prior chapter (Turner 2000). How-ever, project management techniques can also be effective in many sit-uations when complexity steps into the picture. Complexity arises from a variety of sources and leads to complications in the management of projects. When we have a clearly defined goal, then adjustments to the processes of managing the project enable the project manager to drive toward success.

In the course of this chapter, we examine how project managers address the difficulties that arise from complexity. The degree of complex-ity is not dependent on the spectrum of projects. However, complexity is more often associated with projects that require transformation and not those with an established output such as that of installation. Complex projects may involve thousands of project members, detailed contracts with numerous suppliers and clients, a restructuring of production facili-ties, untried technology, multiple sources of knowledge, and replacement of traditional processes and operations. As the project increases in the magnitude of the cost, contains a severe time constraint, requires a variety of technical and operational knowledge, or pursues multiple goals, then the difficulty of the management task is compounded.

One critical assumption we make in this chapter is that the end goals of the project are clearly stated. Even complex transformations often allow this assumption to hold. For example, an automotive manufacturer might require a transformation of assembly facilities to include more artificial intelligence in the assembly during a change in product emphasis from assembling primarily sedans to one of a focus on light trucks and SUVs. Such a transformation will require the application of diverse knowledge across multiple disciplines; installation of new technologies and upgrade of existing machinery; the establishment of new quality control proce-dures and standards; negotiation with employee groups; training of work-ers; and numerous other activities that require spanning significant time, budget, and stakeholders. In such a situation, the complexities are quite large. The approaches to be taken in the achievement of the end goals may not be well understood or fully planned in advance, the members of the team may not be identified adequately at the launch of the project, or the design of the vehicles may adjust between the start and conclusion of the project. However, the desired output is clearly established by top management and communicated throughout the organization providing a well-defined target.

Motivation for Complex Project Management

For the traditional projects described in the prior chapter, universal project management tools (e.g., work breakdown structures and earned value analysis) are all that is necessary to manage the progress of a project. However, when a project launches in complex environments, project managers may find themselves faced with multiple uncertainties of task and timing. These uncertainties directly or indirectly affect the selection of solutions and results and make projects ever more complex. When faced with complexities, project managers often find it difficult to know where to start with a project or may be unable to predict possible risks effectively. If project managers do not make adjustments in process or technique under complex conditions, the odds of completing the required deliverable on time and within budget are reduced.

Clients May Not Know Their Real Needs As Well As You Imagine

The ultimate goal of project management is to fulfill better the demands of clients, those who will work and live with the deliverable. However, in reality, what clients want might not be what they ultimately need. When we listen to clients describing their demands through verbal descriptions, these often only represent what clients want, and only serve as solutions to vague problems that clients might be facing at the current moment. If we accept all that our clients tell us without full verification and use their descriptions as a basis for executing projects, we may belatedly find that situations are more complex than previously imagined. In that case, clients may reject or refuse to utilize our project outputs, pushing the essential product further into the future with greater expenses due to changing scope, repeated tasks, and waste. Further, if a client's needs cannot be accurately defined, solution choice becomes difficult in project execution.

Solution Choices for Complex Projects Are Numerous or Vague

Beyond uncertainties resulting from an absence of exacting requirements, complexities of management inherent in projects also contribute to selection uncertainty of project solutions. In general, each work package or task within a project may have a selection of possible approaches—part of the solution to achieving the product of the project. The uncertainties due to complex conditions remove the potential for one clear approach to any given task. In other words, in the ideal world, we only need to be concerned with the management of critical paths and project progress during project execution to successfully achieve our goals. At times, however, more than one solution approach may be viable for a particular task during project execution leading to different results that affect the remainder of the project.

In Figure 3.1, we see three possible solutions for one of the tasks or work packages in a sample project. Now imagine that there are three work packages within the project with multiple execution methods and solutions, and that these processes are dependent. In other words, the execution method or solution that we choose for the first selection will directly or indirectly affect all processes that follow. Under these circumstances, we can see that there are 27 possible combinations within the project and that the project has now become more complex, confusing the management of critical paths and bottlenecks, as seen in Figure 3.2.

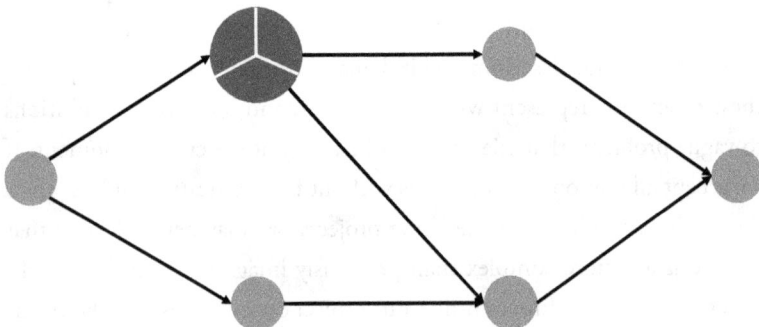

Figure 3.1 A project with three possible solution approaches

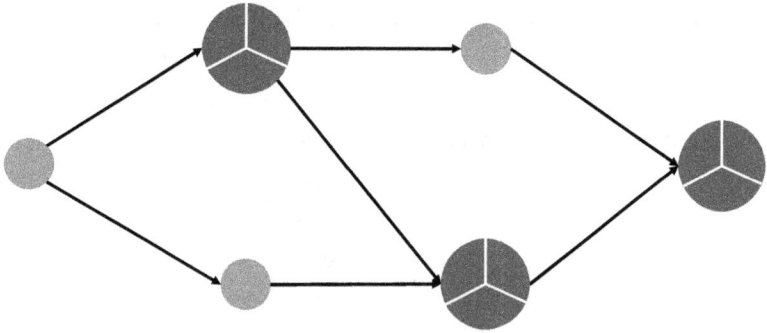

Figure 3.2 A project with 27 possible solution approaches

Let us further imagine for a moment that we expand the scope of this project to that shown in Figure 3.3. The project now contains 2,187 possible solution combinations. We may encounter this complex project in practice. In fact, the projects that we encounter in practice may be even more complex.

When faced with such complex solution combinations, it is impossible to utilize traditional project management techniques without enhancements or adjustments. When client needs are unclear, it is very difficult to

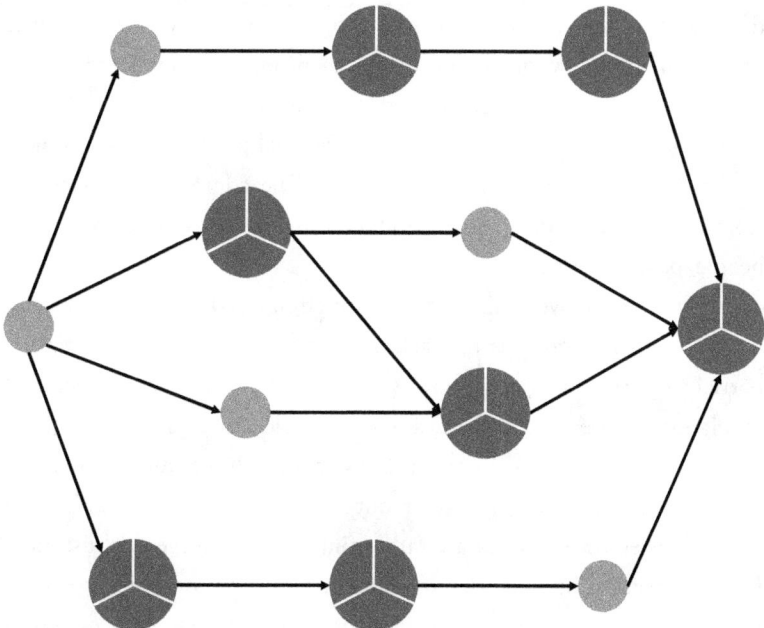

Figure 3.3 A project with 2,187 possible solution approaches

determine the needs of projects, and uncertainty in projects then make it impossible to specify clear solutions or even comprehensive work breakdown structures. The multiple possibilities brought about by the inherent complexities of projects increase the management difficulty. To distinguish traditional projects with clear goals and solution approaches from projects with clear goals but uncertain solution approaches, we use the term "complex projects" for the latter type of projects.

Complex Projects

Consideration of complex projects requires that we examine both the degree and type of complexity. In the prior chapter, we considered projects that had little or no complexity. As projects expand to a greater scope, greater coordination is required to plan required activities and manage the larger team. Even within a single project type, such as construction, the scope or magnitude of the project will change the magnitude of complexity. The design and construction of a single home within a subdivision have minimal complexity. Creating and building a shopping mall has greater complexity, due to the multiuse purpose of the facility as well as the number of different stakeholders, the number of team members, various contracting agencies, and time frame. Even greater complexity would be in the design and construction of an Olympic village with many facilities. Yet still, the final product of each project in these construction examples is defined. The complexity derives not from lack of clarity in the final product as much as the processes, tools, people, or time frame.

At this point, we make a fine distinction between ambiguity and uncertainty. Ambiguity is the lack of a uniform understanding among participants regarding a stated task or objective. A simple version of ambiguity can be seen at the task level. Should a process not be clearly stated, individuals working on the same task might conduct their activities in a fashion such that their outputs will not be compatible. At this task level, the solutions are rather simple through the establishment and clarification of processes to direct activity. At the objective level, this becomes much more severe. The ambiguity of the goals or objectives of a project contradicts the philosophy of project management, which includes deriving a set of task and activities to a well-defined deliverable. If there is no agreement of goals or objectives as a target for project completion, then the establishment of the path to completion becomes a near-impossible task. Additionally, the resolution of ambiguity requires a reach across an organization to other projects, departments, and levels of management. Even though both uncertainty and ambiguity create complexities to exist within projects, we only target those complex projects with management difficulties of uncertainty at this time, limiting ourselves to project goals that tend to be well defined, but for which solutions may be highly complex (Pich, Loch, and Meyer 2002). Projects where ambiguity levels are high cannot be effectively managed through complex project management techniques, but require the utilization of program management concepts presented in the next chapter. To begin, we will categorize sources of complexity that allow for further analysis.

Structural Complexity

Structural complexity derives from the difficulty of managing a large number of different tasks, across numerous departments, with a variety of stakeholders, and is often seen in projects with wide scopes such as transformation projects (Ellinas, Allan, and Johansson 2018). In the example of constructing a shopping mall, many work packages exist that are reliant upon the completion of other activities in the project. This dependency increases the amount of coordination essential in completing a project. The increased number of personnel directly involved with the project require greater attention to the management of human resources. The number of outside contractors increases, adding complexity and difficulty in securing and monitoring the performance of contractual agreements. Overall, the need for coordination among all of the tasks and individuals and stakeholders built into the structure of the project make coordination among all actors highly complex. In other words, the complexities of these projects lie in the management, follow up, and coordination of tasks spread out over multiple departments, stakeholders, and project team members. The main challenges lie in the organization, scheduling, and coordination of actors and tasks.

Technical Complexity

Technical complexity occurs in projects with technical or design issues associated with previously unproduced products or techniques that are unknown or untried and have no precedents, at least within the parent organization. New technology is a common element in the transformation of an organization. Technical complexity is generally seen in architectural, industrial design, or R&D projects, and is common in the chemical and pharmaceutical industries (Kiridena and Sense 2016). In such cases, a specific understanding of the final goal is common, but details of accomplishment and design are not established at the start of the project. In the development of a new medication for the pharmaceutical industry, the goal might be a medication that mitigates the symptoms of Parkinson's disease. However, the courses of action taken to this end might involve one of many practices to include scouring of prior results, derivation of the chemical specifics, testing of efficacy, and pursuit of final commercial approval. Technologies that may affect such a project include the advancing knowledge in the pharmaceutical industry regarding the composition of such medication, computer technologies that assist in the simulation of disease mitigation, and the advancement of laboratory and testing equipment. The main challenge of projects with technical complexities is the lack of specific or clear approaches to arrive at the final product. Such projects must be monitored carefully to determine whether progress is satisfactory, or different approach must be substituted for the initial plans.

Temporal Complexity

Temporal complexity is most often found in projects where external environments change rapidly, such that the project management team must be prepared to respond to unanticipated events. This type of complexity usually stems from the uncertainty of future environments and unpredictable changes, such as changes due to new legislation, major disasters, or the birth of new technologies (Kiridena and Sense 2016). The longer the execution time of a project, the higher the likelihood of running into the governmental, environmental, market, or organizational changes. Temporal complexity is highly correlated to changes external to the project, such as the release of new products by a competitor, tightened labor markets, or corporate mergers, and can occur at any stage of a project's life cycle. All these examples are representative of transformation projects.

Directional Complexity

Directional complexity refers to situations where goals may be unclear, where there is no common goal, where there may be many different descriptions of project goals, or even where there are conflicting goals for different stakeholders—all these forms create ambiguity about the desired finality (Kiridena and Sense 2016). The challenge of directional complexity is to move toward organizational objectives when the objective target has no common meaning across stakeholder groups. For example, in the implementation of an enterprise system for an organization, each functional manager might have different expectations of the benefits. Marketing staff might consider the ability to conduct business analytics of the customer base as a primary goal while operations professionals intend to enjoy a closer tie to associates of the supply chain. Though there is obvious overlap, the goals are dissimilar requiring different alignment of duties both during the implementation and in the operations after implementation. Transformation often leads to ill-defined goals or differences in the understanding of final expectations of the new strategy or direction.

The Basis of Complex Project Management

Project management focuses on delivering a specific outcome. To that end, the perspective of a project manager considers several important aspects for successful completion, as highlighted in Table 3.1. For a traditional project, the targeted deliverable is clearly defined. That is not to say the means of achievement is defined; processes for achievement are often left to the project manager or the project team (Pich, Loch, and Meyer 2002). Project success is evaluated through adherence to the budget, schedule, and scope of the output, which includes quality aspects. Note that this success consideration is for the project in isolation of the organization; the organization will be more interested in the success of the output that must meet expectations of value.

Table 3.1 Focal aspects of project management

Targeted deliverable	Clear, defined deliverable
Performance criteria	Cost, time, scope, quality
Change flexibility	Avoid change
Interaction	Related to tasks, product delivery
Control	Compare actuals to schedules, budgets, and specifications
Orientation	Define and complete work, manage teams and risks

Changes during a project require flexibility. However, a project that is set up for specific requirements of cost, time, and scope suffers in the face of change. Minor changes to a project might fall within allowed variances established at the beginning of the project. More substantial changes, however, require replanning, reassessment, and new approvals before continuing to completion. Interactions with the stakeholders, including team members and sponsors, are mostly related to acquiring essential information to complete the required tasks and secure necessary resources along with information regarding the status of the final product delivery (Chua et al. 2012). Controls over the project progress are primarily conducted through variance comparisons to the planned schedule, budget, staffing, and deliverable specification (Wiener et al. 2016). The orientation of managerial duties focuses on the detailed planning activities required to complete the work, managing the staff, and monitoring for anticipated and unanticipated risks.

However, as project managers find their projects contain one or more complexities, the aspects become more complicated. The performance criteria will not change at the project level, though continual refinement may be necessary. Flexibility comes in through the selection of different solution approaches requiring early selection, with the possibility of some alteration based upon the presence of multiple paths to completion. The aspects of interaction, control, and orientation must adjust to the complexities inherent in the project. Unless great care is taken, some aspects of the project will be neglected or allowed to develop on their own. This isolation often occurs as organizations simplify projects to secure greater control, at least in appearance if not in fact. However, to fully attend to all aspects of a project, the identification of key tasks, and the allocation of resources and effort become more important and require complex project management.

Complex Project Management

Research and practice extend along a spectrum of responses to complexity. Figure 3.4 illustrates this simple consideration. At the low end of the spectrum, complexities are simply paved over, and all projects treated similarly. Such a perspective falls from the early consideration of project management, where a common template could be applied to all project situations. This end is unrealistic, as the failure to consider complexities will lead to disastrous results. At the other end of the spectrum, each condition of complexity is regarded as a unique problem that requires a unique response. This is typical of scientific research that requires isolation of a particular problem to conduct a legitimate study (Bakhshi, Ireland, and Zubielqui 2015). This end of the spectrum is also unrealistic, as consideration of every individual complexity and resulting situations would require analysis beyond the capacity of an organization. In between the extremes, we can rely on the knowledge of complexity, consider the potential impact, and take a realistic approach to the development of project plans and progress. For each level and categorization of complexity, we can establish a set of guidelines.

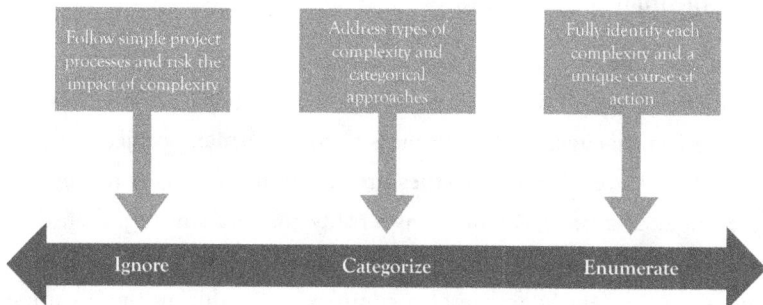

Figure 3.4 Responses to complexity

Conducting Complex Project Management

From figures 3.1 to 3.3, we were able to provide a brief understanding of complex projects based on the increased number of solution approaches. However, in practice, projects may be so complex that there may not be clear solutions. To better understand this, we can divide the complexities of projects into two dimensions: problem space and solution space. When executing complex projects, we identify problems that require solving. Usually, there will be more than one, and these problems will then form a problem space. In the same way, when faced with complex issues, we may find that there is more than one solution, and these solutions form a solution space. When executing projects, we can utilize the correlations between the problem space and the solution space of complex components to find solutions that solve the greatest number of problems within the problem space, and at the same time ensure that chosen solutions do not exceed project budgets. Firms operating under constraints set by limited resources must identify solutions within both the problem and solution spaces that solve the greatest number of problems with the fewest resources spent on the chosen solution. Since complexities establish more problems but also provide more possible solution approaches, we must find the best approach from a larger number of possibilities. We strive for techniques that rely on the middle of the response spectrum in Figure 3.4. We must first determine which complexities are present, then consider the aspects of interaction, control, and orientation.

Identification of Complexities

The first thing we must do when faced with a complex project is to identify the complexities present within the project. A review of previous project management experiences shows that many project managers only discover the complexities present within a project during the late stages of a project, when it is already too late since by then they may have lost control of the project (Baccarini 1996). Therefore, the best time to identify and resolve complexities is during the planning stages of a project. If we realize that complexities may be present within a project, we can then address them early in the early stages of the project. This identification is also appropriate for assessments conducted before each subsequent stage of a project to confirm whether project complexities still exist, or if new complexities have arisen. Complexities may be identified with a set of simple questions that may not have simple answers. These appear in Table 3.2. The answers to these questions can then be judged to complete an evaluation matrix, such as the one shown in Table 3.3. It is important to stress that this assessment should be repeated at the beginning of every stage in a project's life cycle. Different complexities may arise at different stages of a project. Using this complexity matrix, we can identify appropriate complex project management tools to manage interactions, control, and orientation effectively.

Table 3.2 Questions to identify complexity

Structural Complexity
1. What is the scope of the project?
2. How many suppliers, contractors, and subcontractors will be involved?
3. How many different departments in the organization will be impacted?
4. Are there many independent activities present in the project (or for each stage)?
5. Does the budget require a substantial allocation from organizational sources?
6. Will resources be primarily dedicated or shared with other projects or departments?
Technical Complexity
1. Are there innovative design expectations?
2. Is the project team clear on how to structure and complete the project?
3. Has the organization experience using the technology involved?
4. Does the technology to complete the project exist in-house?
5. Are there any related technology projections that might alter the choice of technology?
Temporal Complexity
1. Does the project have a clear activation or onboard date?
2. Is the project dependent on political and environmental issues?
3. Does the risk analysis indicate issues that may arise to delay the entire project?
4. Is delivery dependent on external suppliers or contractors?
5. Does the project extend into subsequent fiscal periods?
6. Are there any planned reorganizations in the near future?

Table 3.3 Project complexity matrix

Complexity	Low	Medium	High
Structural (Number of independent elements)			
Technical (Impact of unresolved technical or design issues)			
Temporal (Extended time horizons in a project)			

Processes of Complex Project Management

After identifying the project complexities, we must consider how to manage each type of complexity from the viewpoint of the aforementioned three aspects (interaction, control, and orientation) for complex project management.

Structurally Complex Projects

Let us first look at projects with structural complexities. These types of projects constantly focus on questions such as, "How can we coordinate all the involved departments?" or "How can we follow up on department correlations?" (Davies, and Mackenzie 2014; Peng, Heim, and Mallick 2014). As we already mentioned, structural complexities are often seen in projects with wide scope. In projects with structural complexities, a challenge we often face is being unable to conceptualize the entire scope of the project. Here, it is difficult to coordinate all of the people, tasks, and items when forecasting a project time line (Ellinas, Allan, and Johansson 2018, p. 236). Resources across simultaneous and emerging tasks become difficult as the number of tasks increases.

Figure 3.5 is a graphical representation of structural complexity. The figure represents a certain point in time for a project with structural complexity, where uncertainty is present in seven segments chosen as solution approaches but having uncertainties regarding timing, cost, and resource coordination. Likewise, for this project, there will be a problem space and a solution space from which the solution segments were chosen. Constraints may exist, represented by the fixed shape in the bottom left corner, perhaps being specific demands of clients, constraints imposed by external

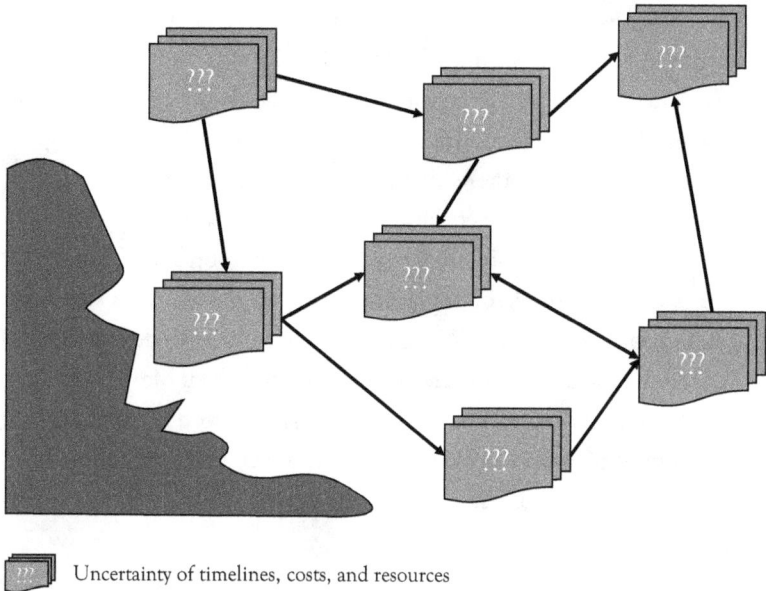

??? Uncertainty of timelines, costs, and resources

Figure 3.5 A structurally complex project

environments, or even constraints of time lines, resources, and budgets. Even if we are able to predict the scope, time, budget, and demands of a project precisely, an event or change in any segment of a project can derail the entire project. This is because projects with structural complexity have too many connections among the solution segments chosen to meet requirements.

With clearly defined problem and solution spaces in hand, we can plan the execution of the interconnected segments of a project. For each aspect:

Interaction Aspect. In structurally complex projects, interactions are typically channeled through rule-bound communication paths. This approach is a highly formal communication arrangement where information filters according to certain rules to facilitate effective communication. The system focuses on standardized information, and all other information is ignored. This method of information processing makes it easy for the entire system to respond rapidly to information triggers. A rigid communication plan that adheres to defined communication paths is an effective tool.

Control aspect. In structurally complex projects, the internal behaviors of a project must be inflexible, in that the roles of all participants and their responsibilities must be clearly defined, and the modes of interaction must remain intact from the beginning of the project until the end. In terms of internal management, management items are very clear and detailed, so that it is possible to achieve rigorous and stable control. Standard operating procedures are an example of management techniques used for structurally complex projects. Work packages must be fully defined for time and cost, and progress recorded and monitored. Most importantly, projects must undergo stage evaluations to determine the stability of plans as any changes severely affect a great number of resources and outcomes.

Orientation Aspect. The main orientation for structurally complex projects is one with a clear reporting hierarchy. In general, the implementation, interaction, and control systems of a project are highly formal in management structure, with clear segmentation of duties between different solution segments. The management structure of the military may serve as a pattern with its clearly defined authority, assigned responsibility, and multiple layers in the hierarchies. Responsibility matrices are effective planning devices to document this rigidity. Flexibility is minimized, and slack often disappears due to interconnected solution segments that feed one another. The planned use and exchange of shared resources should be limited as any issue in one activity will spill into another.

Technically Complex Projects

In contrast with structurally complex projects, technically complex projects are focused on questions such as, "How can we solve this technical or design issue?," "Has anyone ever done this before?," or "What methods can we apply to complete this project or produce a product?"

Technical complexities often arise in the design process for new products or the development process for new technologies (Kiridena and Sense 2016). Although we can reference similar projects conducted in the past when making decisions about a new project, it is fruitless to make decisions on the main issues of technically complex projects. In practice, we may find that some projects with technical complexities are unable to produce any products by the end of the project, or that the issues of the project can never be reasonably resolved (Ahern, Leavy, and Byrne 2014).

Because there is no recognized standard for solutions in technically complex projects, it is often difficult to identify a solution space, and therefore, project team members are continuously searching for better solutions. Satisfaction levels for solutions are often hard to assess as they depend highly on the individual. Unlike structural complexities, the breadth of scope may not be an indicator. Technical complexities can appear in projects of any scope, and uncertainties usually appear in the solution-seeking process where potential solutions may also affect the interconnected segments of projects. Technical complexities often open the solution space to a greater number of approaches, making specific choices more difficult. Further, technical solutions may drastically alter results, changing the output at each work package, and altering the input to successive steps. We again consider the three aspects of complex project management to technically complex projects:

Interaction aspect. In technically complex projects, methods of internal communication may be varied. Interaction often occurs in informal meetings or discussions, and important information is typically communicated over informal channels. In contrast with structurally complex projects, communication channels for technically complex projects tend to be less structured and less regulated, and there is often no clear boundary between formal and informal communication channels.

The strength and frequency of information exchange are often circular in technically complex projects. During periodic follow-up meetings or production meetings, the strength and frequency of information exchange tend to rise significantly, though communication tends to return to usual modes in future stages as groups return to their positions to work on dedicated tasks.

As technically complex projects tend to have many autonomous groups, risks may arise if timely and effective interaction is not facilitated between groups, and some groups may believe that their tasks and goals are consistent with those of other groups, while in actuality their focus may have shifted from the main goal of the project. For this reason, mechanisms of formal exchanges must be installed and informal exchanges encouraged but documented.

Control Aspect. Technically complex projects are controlled through intergroup interaction, which maintains consistency and accuracy of project directions. Timely and effective information exchanged is maintained through periodic meetings, ensuring that the focus of all groups is consistent and accurate. When changes in external environments make it necessary to alter project plans, reorganizational meetings similar to the original kickoff logically follow.

Technically complex projects are mostly innovative projects that rely on innovative ideas and suggestions, and periodic meetings can seek out or assess these ideas and suggestions. Finally, periodic meetings can ensure that all groups are working to the same schedule, as autonomy may sometimes lead to situations where each group is too focused on its work and thus ignores external information. Thus, controls are more clan-based, as it is through regulation by others that the project stays on track.

Orientation Aspect. In technically complex projects, it is necessary to develop a flat organizational orientation as the participants in this type of project tend to possess high levels of professional expertise and also attach great importance to their autonomy. Team members should be assigned to different functional groups according to differences in project tasks, and the leaders of these functional groups should be given greater levels of freedom. Leaders in these groups are often tagged informally over time, so when managing this type of orientation, we need to understand the role of each team member. As groups are divided by function, work boundaries are relatively clear, and these groups are usually able to maintain internal order and progress with minimal validation. The management of each group may differ depending on the nature of each group, as each group will form suitable operational modes according to their own needs. Therefore, managers do not need to codify strict regulations or impose rigidity on these groups. What we should be concerned about is whether these groups are receiving appropriate support from upper managers when executing their tasks.

Temporally Complex Projects

A temporally complex project focuses on questions such as, "How can we predict, survive, or achieve advantages in an ever-changing environment?" or "How can we adjust projects to changing environments?" Temporal complexity often arises when projects face major external environmental changes (Kiridena and Sense 2016). Even when we anticipate major changes, we are often unable to predict when or where the changes will occur. In the private sector, temporal complexities often appear during mergers, leadership changes, or organizational restructurings. In the public sector, temporal complexities often result from changes in laws and regulations (Ramus, Vaccaro, and Stefano 2017). For temporally complex projects, an accurate grasp of all time points and positioning of time points is essential. At each time point, the output must satisfy the needs of the emerging environment.

Temporal complexity often coincides with structural complexity as an enlarged scope is often accompanied by a longer time horizon. Technical complexity also has implications in temporal complexity as the rapidity of technological advances opens a broader solution space during a project. Further temporal complexities arise from the combined impact of different elements, connections between elements, and uncertainties in project elements. Even though there may be a correspondence between temporal and the other complexities, temporal complexities stem from different sources.

Temporal complexity does not arise from the high number of interconnected elements as in structural complexity, nor from multiple solution options due to technical complexity, but from constraints. In structurally complex and technically complex projects, constraints are regarded as stable from the project definition stage. However, constraints are a factor that must be considered for temporally complex projects, such as whether additional constraints will appear, existing constraints disappear, or unstable constraints morph in the project environment with time. However, the problem and solution spaces of a temporally complex project, exclusive of other complexities, can be clearly defined at the beginning of a project, even though these too may change with time. Systems within a temporally complex project will change constantly with time. In other words, temporally complex projects will not reach ultimate equilibrium.

When managing temporally complex projects, there may be a conflict with traditional project management tools. Traditional project management tools assume the project environment to be stable, which is at odds with temporally complex projects. In temporally complex projects, what we focus on is not how these changes affect project goals, but when these changes occur, what changes will occur, whether we can face the challenges brought on by environmental changes, or if it is even possible to seize deliverable-oriented opportunities due to environmental changes. We discuss temporally complex projects from the three aspects of complex project management:

Interaction aspect. In temporally complex projects, varied methods of interaction play an important role in maintaining the internal order of a project. Information exchanges are frequent and initiated through informal paths as the identification of changes can arise from many sources. However, communication of any change to the project still requires dissemination to the entire team, suggesting formal structures are required. Project stakeholders and project team members all need a full understanding of the situation at hand. In this way, on the one hand, we obtain insights regarding responses to changes in project environments, insights that project team members may be hard put to observe. On the other hand, if project team members fail to understand changes in project environment changes fully, those responsible for specific tasks within the team may abandon ongoing tasks due to new constraints, and team members may suffer the consequences of partially completed tasks. Therefore, stakeholders and team members need to be acutely aware of any changes in project environments.

Control aspect. In contrast to structurally complex and directionally complex projects, temporally complex projects tend to have a clear transition stage: in most projects with temporal complexities, all tasks are assigned and attended to in the beginning, until project environments begin to change and form different constraints. Then, the project will undergo a transition period where internal tasks that are simultaneously ongoing have to be paused. All project resources must be concentrated on project tasks that are most suited to the current project environment, making it possible to achieve desired results. Here we can see the difference between temporally complex projects and traditional projects. Temporally complex projects need to deliver suitable results at a correct point in time, rather than complete within a certain period. Because of this, it is difficult to plan project schedules for temporally complex projects. Attention should focus on whether it is possible to achieve project goals and deliver suitable project results at a certain point in time based on the external environments of a project.

Orientation aspect. In general, project managers must juggle multiple options during the execution of a project. This action indicates many tasks may be simultaneously ongoing and many segments within a project may be very similar to other segments. Project team members must be independent, but also collaborate as they search for a project theme, in the same manner that jazz musicians remain independent yet collaborative when playing a piece. When executing temporally complex projects, it is best not to have just one person focusing on possible solutions: everyone needs to understand the possible solutions for each project. In this way, when external environments of projects change and render any one solution impossible, the change will not wipe out the contribution of any single project member. It is best to ensure that all solutions are openly available until proven that a particular solution is no longer feasible and needs removal from the solution space. In this way, we provide situations where project team members have the opportunity to promote better solutions.

Limitations and Challenges of Complex Project Management

The complex project management discussed in this chapter provides the project manager with advice on adjustments to traditional project management techniques to deal with complexity. These conceptually simple adjustments help an organization better cope with structural, technological, and temporal complexity to improve performance, but limitations still exist in terms of specific methodologies and directional complexity. The challenge lies in developing specific methods beyond those of traditional project management and approaches to the more difficult situation of ambiguity in the goals of transformation.

Effective Identification of Project Complexity

Direct consideration of project complexity allows for identification through straightforward questions that surface potential complexities. In addition to general questions, inquiries directed at specific contexts or even organizations may be an important aspect of complexity identification.

Such methods to evaluate the need for adjustments to traditional approaches may be overly simplistic. As with most methods in the practice of project management, suggested identification approaches to date target reducing complexities to simplistic representations, often through documentation or segmentation. Thus, the signs of complexity may be overlooked or disguised. Further, approaches to analyzing the complexity of a project lean to qualitative criteria, there are no standards of a quantitative nature. Therefore, when we judge the complexity of a project, it is likely that the subjective consciousness of the evaluator and the experience of the project manager will influence any judgment.

Adjustments to Project Approaches Under Complexity

Advice regarding adjustments to the project management process is overly simplistic, typically stressing the need to alter lines of communication, add more controls, and rely more on the talent of the team. However, it regularly happens that more than one type of complexity exists in a project, and the advice may be conflicting across types. For example, structural complexity tends to advise rigid channels of information exchange, while technological complexity moves toward informal lines of exchange. In such a case, allowing the informal exchange is critical, but so is the capture of the exchange for documentation and dissemination.

When Ambiguity Encroaches

Complex project management adjusts traditional approaches under structural, technological, or temporal complexities. Even when the scope of a project is extensive, the path to completion unresolved, or significant environmental changes are possible, complex project management adjustments apply. However, one of the prerequisites for effective management of such projects is that the project goals and objectives are specific. A direction to completion is evident even if uncertainty clouds the solution space. When the project goal becomes blurred or not commonly understood, the corresponding project work no longer has a clear direction.

Putting a man on the moon was a very specific goal that transformed a great deal of scientific understanding and engineering practice, but the complexities were extensive. A goal stated as the exploration of space, however, lacks any specifics. Yet space exploration continues to transform how we view our environment and expand our scientific knowledge, and the effort is a collection of many complex projects. Organizations face smaller transformations but still deal with matters of survival in a future environment that cannot be adequately quantified into precise goals and objectives. Goal ambiguity derives from a lack of goals, imprecise goals, or difference among stakeholders in their understanding of goals. The lack of direction, directional complexity, requires one consider comprehensive techniques. These will include program management and project portfolio management.

Discussion Questions

1. Identify three risks and three uncertainties faced when planning a backpacking vacation through Europe. How would you mitigate the risks? Why would those mitigations not address the uncertainties?
2. Does technical complexity typically increase as structural complexity increases?
3. Would the organizational structure in your organization, or a well-known organization, allow for adequate interactions in temporally complex projects?
4. Answer the questions in Table 3.2 for any project in your organization or any well-publicized public project (such as the construction of a government web portal). Would you feel comfortable in your assessment of the table in Figure 3.3 for that project? Explain.
5. Why does ambiguity create havoc for project managers?

Reference

Ahern, T., B. Leavy, and P.J. Byrne. 2014. "Complex Project Management as Complex Problem Solving: A Distributed Knowledge Management Perspective." *International Journal of Project Management* 32, no. 8, pp. 1371–1381. doi: 10.1016/j.ijproman.2013.06.007

Baccarini, D. 1996. "The Concept of Project Complexity—A Review."

International Journal of Project Management 14, no. 4, 201–204. doi: 10.1016/0263-7863(95)00093-3

Bakhshi, J., V. Ireland, and G.C. De Zubielqui. 2015. "Exploring Project Complexities: A Critical Review of the Literature." AIPM National Conference, Australia, Hobart.

Chua, C.E., W.K. Lim, C. Soh, and S.K. Sia. 2012. "Enacting Clan Control in Complex IT Projects: A Social Capital Perspective." *MIS Quarterly* 36, no. 2, 577–600. doi: 10.2307/41703468.

Davies, A., and I. Mackenzie. 2014. "Project Complexity and Systems Integration: Constructing the London 2012 Olympics and Paralympics Games." *International Journal of Project Management* 32, no. 5, 773–790. doi: 10.1016/j.ijproman.2013.10.004

Ellinas, C., N. Allan, and A. Johansson. 2018. "Toward Project Complexity Evaluation: A Structural Perspective." *IEEE Systems Journal* 12, no. 1, 228–239. doi: 10.1109/JSYST.2016.2562358

Kiridena, S., and A. Sense, A. 2016. "Profiling Project Complexity: Insights from Complexity Science and Project Management Literature." *Project Management Journal* 47, no. 6, 56–74. doi: 10.1177/875697281604700605

Peng, D.X., G.R. Heim, and D.N. Mallick. 2014. "Collaborative Product Development: The Effect of Project Complexity on the Use of Information Technology Tools and New Product Development Practices." *Production and Operations Management* 23, no. 8, 1421–1438. doi: 10.1111/j.1937-5956.2012.01383.x

Pich, M.T., C.H. Loch, and A. De Meyer. 2002. "On Uncertainty, Ambiguity, and Complexity in Project Management." *Management Science* 48, no. 8, 1008–1023. doi:10.1287/mnsc.48.8.1008.163

Ramus, T., A. Vaccaro, and S. Brusoni. 2017. "Institutional Complexity in Turbulent Times: Formalization, Collaboration, and the Emergence of Blended Logics." *Academy of Management Journal* 60, no. 4, 1253–1284. doi:10.5465/amj.2015.0394

Turner, J.R. 2000. "Do You Manage Work, Deliverables, or Resources?" *International Journal of Project Management* 18, no. 2, 83–84. doi: 10.1016/s0263-7863(99)00059-9

Wiener, M., M. Mähring, U. Remus, and C. Saunders. 2016. "Control Configuration and Control Enactment in Information Systems Projects: Review and Expanded Theoretical Framework." *MIS Quarterly* 40, no. 3, 741–774. doi: 10.25300/MISQ/2016/40.3.11

CHAPTER 4

Program Management

- Uncertainty refers to the means to achieve outcomes, whereas ambiguity refers to the degree of change in goals over time.
- Program management aims to govern project sets in uncertain and ambiguous environments to achieve synergy and pursue strategic ideals.
- Program management is concerned with the integration of multiple project deliverables to maximize opportunities inherent in change.
- Transformations to meet ambiguous goals in an uncertain future exceed the capabilities of traditional project management.

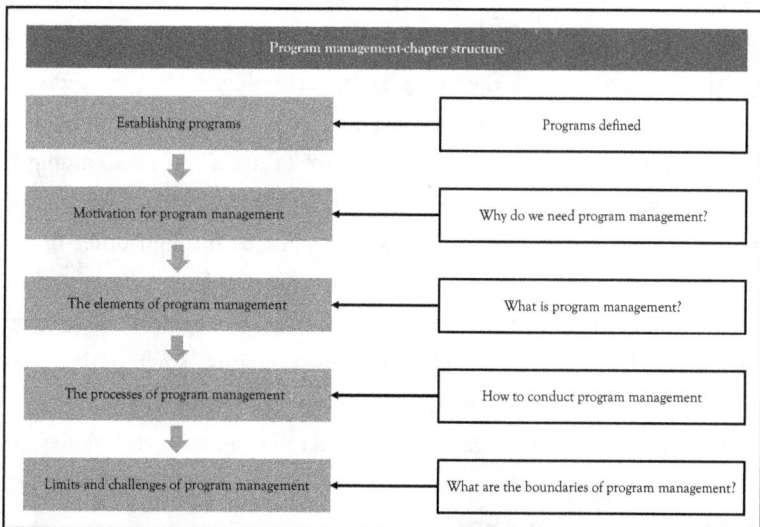

Chapter Structure

What Is a Program?

A program is a set of interconnected projects, all pursuing a benefit not achievable through a single project (PMI 2017). The Managing Successful Programs framework defines programs as "temporary organizations established to coordinate, command, and monitor a group of related projects, where the goal is to produce outcomes and benefits consistent with organizational strategic goals (OGC 2011)." Programs require a series of transformational activities (projects and operational activities) integrated to realize benefits of a common goal, where it is possible to identify significant connections and coordination effects between all activities and stakeholders. These coordinated projects, when integrated with operations, bring lasting and stable benefits to an organization, whereas if even one project lacks a core vision and a clear goal, intended objectives may not be achieved, and may overlap or conflict with other projects.

Due to the ever-increasing complexity of projects, many studies classify projects based on metrics such as goals versus means, levels of uncertainty, or complexities (Thiry 2002; Thiry 2004; Thiry 2010; Jiang et al. 2014; Chang et al. 2014). There are many similarities between complex projects and programs. However, despite programs being more complex than projects, many people still think of programs as extended or large projects, where the same tools, technologies, and concepts of projects are applicable in the management and control of the program. This misconception stems from a confusion of uncertainty and ambiguity. High uncertainty does not result in high directional complexity but makes projects more difficult to manage, perhaps through other forms of complexity (Pich et al. 2002). If projects are ambiguous because they are not clearly defined or because they have a high degree of directional complexity, they should be implemented as programs. When project outputs cannot be clearly defined at the onset because of high ambiguity or directional complexity, traditional project management techniques are improper, and implementation must be facilitated through a program management perspective.

A common example of a program is the installation of a complex enterprise system (ES). One common goal of an organizationwide

BI Goal set

SCM Goal set   CRM Goal set

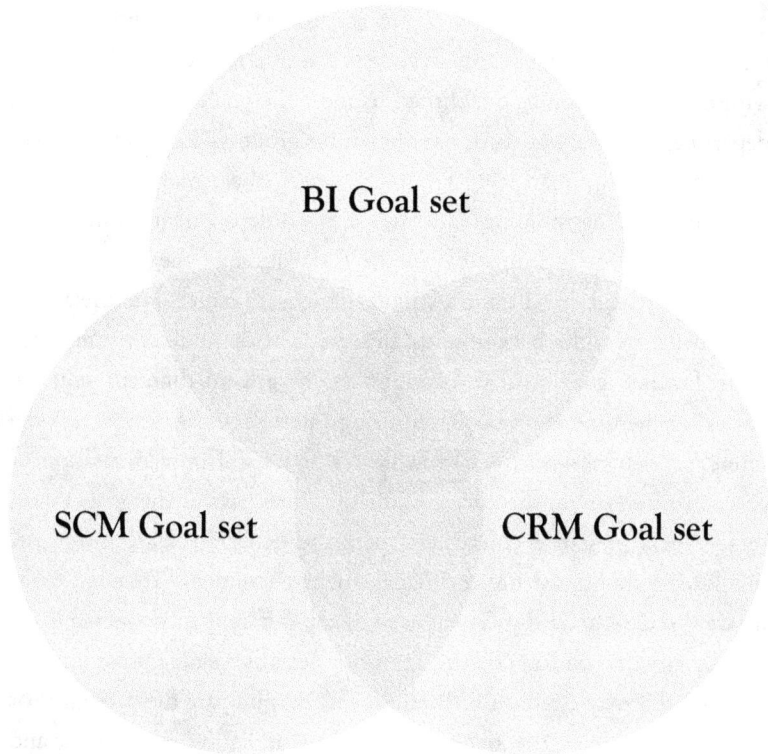

Figure 4.1 Enterprise system goals

enterprise information system is the standardization, integration, and availability of data across all functional areas within the organization and in a secure fashion to external partners as required. Figure 4.1 illustrates the unique aspect of an ES within an organization. The organization as a whole expects benefits from the installation of the ES with goals established that reflect the interests of each functional area. However, stakeholders in the marketing department might see specific advantages for information sharing across the organization, such as the ability to coordinate sales with production capability for better delivery promises to customers. The marketing group will further expect functionality to support customer relationship management activity. On the other hand, the operations stakeholders will look forward to coordinating data efforts for the management of their supply chain. Still, others in the organization will have their main interest in the business intelligence functions of the enterprise system.

If considered individually, a project associated with supply chain management in an ES might have very specific deliverables associated with data integration as established to meet the goals of the operations department. Certain goals of the operations group will certainly overlap with those of the marketing group. However, there may also be goals that have nothing in common across the two departments, which may be compatible or incompatible in the installation of the system. Even those goals held in common might present different interpretations dependent upon the backgrounds and needs of the different functional areas. Further, goals held in common might present different solution spaces for the different groups, requiring careful coordination across the interdependent projects. Yet to achieve a successful implementation of an enterprise system, the ambiguities and differences of the goals for all stakeholders present a condition where the deliverables are imprecise, disallowing traditional project management techniques. Thus, an organization establishes a project for each of the different components in an ES implementation but coordinates all projects as a single program. The organization may establish further projects that prepare the personnel or suppliers to employ the systems, build out the hardware required, and alter any legacy systems to prepare for conversion.

Programs typically arise in the transformation of an organization (Martinsuo and Hoverfält 2018). Transformations may be simplistic and require only a project for implementation, such as a project for launching a new employee onboarding process. However, transformations quickly increase in complexity, including directional complexity. An organization may require transformation to penetrate new markets, to implement new quality control systems at multiple levels in the organization, to alter a culture to become more consumer oriented, or adjust to new legislation or social expectations. An organization dedicating to a new quality control philosophy may require new technology platforms, employee behaviors, and manufacturing equipment. Many projects would result. As early projects are completed, the deliverables of each project often serve in the determination of the next projects launched. Resource allocation instills dependencies across projects as personnel, cash, and facilities are limited. The interdependency of tasks, resources, and goals, along with the ambiguity of higher level goals or measurement of goals, is what characterizes a program. The benefits of such a quality control program might be numerous, difficult to quantify, and be perceived differently by the different functional areas. A program is accomplished through multiple projects that have autonomy of completion and clarity of goals, even if the projects have other forms of complexity such as temporal, structural, or technological.

The Motivation for Program Management

With environmental changes, the scope of project management and complex project management becomes ever wider, and more and more managers come to find that in practice, one is gradually conscious of "project collections." The reason for combining projects is that when projects are managed together, managers find that certain "chemical reactions" may occur, and benefits that cannot be realized when managing individual projects can be found (Ferns 1991; PMI 2017). As earlier alluded, the biggest difference between project collections and projects lies in uncertainty and ambiguity, and the different risk avoidance viewpoints between traditional and complex project management. In project collections, the risk avoidance perspective is closer to that of Peter Drucker's position on strategic efficiency, where the focus lies in maximizing opportunities and not in minimizing risks (Thiry 2002; Thiry 2004). The core of program management lies in finding benefits and opportunities to generate value from uncertainty and ambiguity. Because of this difference, we are required to apply a new set of management systems and techniques when managing project collections as programs (Pellegrinelli 2011). If organizations continue to utilize techniques of traditional project management or complex project management, they risk losses of opportunity, value, and benefits.

Loss of Opportunity to Integrate Strategy

Project collections often exist in complex environments. Continually changing environments make it difficult for managers to establish clear strategic goals before the execution of project collections, and, therefore, managers need to consider emerging strategies apart from existing strategic plans. When program managers are planning baseline strategies according to actual conditions, they can later adjust and optimize strategic plans as helpful for obtaining and increasing final benefits. Managers are no longer followers of strategy, but rather drivers and developers of organizational strategic goals. This type of management technique is ideal for organizational strategic transformation. Traditional project management techniques are only concerned with how to accomplish specific plans, and therefore lack flexibility in attaining strategic goals. However, high levels of uncertainty and ambiguity in project collections require continued assessment and flexible management strategies. From this perspective, application of traditional project management techniques in the management of project collections will result in loss of opportunities to integrate strategy, which will then result in failure due to falling into a project management mode.

Loss of Potential Value and Benefits

In practice, the choice of traditional project management techniques is subjective and mostly concerned with whether one's projects are successful. However, in project collections, it is necessary for all personnel to think in terms of "our" success. Compared to traditional projects assessed on whether or not they deliver the expected scope on time and budget, programs find this type of assessment lacks in foresight and negates potential opportunities to generate value. Project collections must change their products on the fly based on the benefits gained by the organization. Program stakeholders can only identify potential value in project collections and go on to find additional benefits to an organization when given enough motivation and autonomy to do so (Thiry 2002). Thus, project management techniques and cultures do not apply where there is a high level of ambiguity. Unlike traditional project management, program management is an innovative management concept and culture with complex systemic perspectives, is value and benefit oriented, and encourages continuous learning for proper directional change.

A systemic perspective is a core element of program management (Maylor et al. 2006). Programs are characterized by uncertainty, and program management is made up of systems where strategic decisions are made at a program level to better meet the demands of organizational executives, managers, and project teams. Development of a comprehensive viewpoint of project planning and project reporting addresses better complex external environments and complex project collection structures. The focus of management lies in maximizing benefits, in communicating among key stakeholders, and in coordinating between projects. Systemic coordination can transform the complexities of project collections in the program into opportunities to generate benefits for a company.

The end objectives of program management are value and benefit oriented. When determining the success of programs, final program benefits are the key deliverable. Reaction to opportunities that increase final benefits weaken persistence toward the generation of planned deliverables during the program, increasing flexibility to pursue enhanced value. Reacting to the uncertainty and ambiguity of programs makes continued learning a natural imperative during the management process (Dutton 2014). Only through continued learning, will we grasp the emerging goals of a program or even understand the connections among individual projects and a large, diverse set of stakeholders. Making adjustments over time requires learning from the environment and the early projects. Only through continued learning will organizations achieve ultimate strategic goals, obtaining expected (or perhaps even more than expected) values and benefits from transitional programs.

The Elements of Program Management

Although program management has been widely discussed throughout industry and by academic scholars, there is still no unified definition or practice set for program management. This has, to some extent, created ambiguity in program management itself. In order to manage and integrate a collection of projects to achieve the expected business benefits and create value for stakeholders, organizations typically form a program team to ensure consistency across the strategic goals of the program and the organization, as well as the objectives of various business units. The program team must serve the interests of the organization and work across levels to include executive levels, functional managers, and project managers.

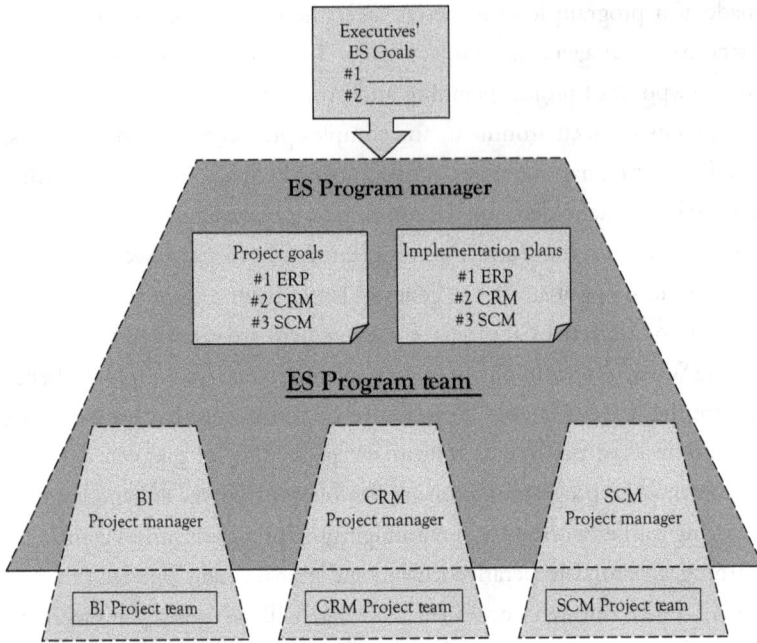

Figure 4.2 Enterprise system program team

Figure 4.2 is a simplified representation of a program team for the earlier ES example. The strategy of the organization is set in goals by the executives. The goals are provided to the ES program team encapsulating the benefits to be achieved. This may be one goal, such as the integration of data across all functional areas, or have additional goals such as operational efficiency. A program manager will lead the ES program team. Further members of the team will include the project managers from all included projects. Other members may represent specific functional areas, technology expertise, or ES consultants. The program team works within the constraints of the goals established by the executives and the resources available to the program for completion. Each project will have a defined deliverable to include scope, budget, and schedule that moves the organization forward in attainment of the overarching ES goals. At this time, each project may bring in goals specific to local interests as long as they have no conflict with the goals of the organization or other projects. Goals are thus set for all the projects; and implementation plans for each project established to consider the interdependencies among projects. The project managers then assume autonomous control over their contribution to the completion of the program. During the entire duration of the program, projects are subject to change, elimination, or addition to meet a change in the environment or understanding of the program.

Moving From Project Management to Program Management

Project management focuses on outputs and performance, and program management focuses on the realization of organizational benefits and learning-based management. Project interdependencies in complex environments and management of various activities in highly predictable conditions require very different management techniques. Therefore, process flows and knowledge systems of project management cannot be applied directly to program management. Consider the distinctions indicated in Table 4.1. Rather than specifying a specific deliverable, the targets become business benefits. Attaining those benefits becomes the primary evaluation of performance for the program. For projects, change is to be avoided, while programs must monitor the environment and organization

Table 4.1 Focal aspects of project and program management

Aspect	Projects	Programs
Targeted Deliverable	Clear, defined deliverable	Defined business benefits
Performance Criteria	Cost, time, scope, quality	Attainment of benefits
Change Flexibility	Avoid change	Capitalize on change
Interaction	Related to tasks, product delivery	Related to pacing and coordination of projects, delivery of benefits
Control	Compare actuals with schedules, budgets, and specifications	Compare delivered benefits to expectations, continual assessment of projects
Orientation	Define and complete work, manage teams and risks	Market the program, monitor the environment

Table 4.2 Moving from project management to program management

From Projects	To Programs
Integrated management	Decision management
Scope management	Value management
Time management	Pace management
Cost management	Resource management
Quality management	Benefits management
Stakeholder management	Elevated stakeholder management
Communication management	Marketing management
Risk management	Uncertainty management
Procurement management	Partner relations and value chain management

for changes that present opportunities. The interactions held among the stakeholders and team members focus on the capitalization of the benefits for the organization and the coordination of all projects within the program. Controlling a program requires that the benefits be measured in some fashion and compared to expectations established at launch. The delivery of value must be assessed continually to determine the mixture of projects, which can change accordingly. The orientation of a program is to monitor the environment for changes that present opportunities or threats and to market the program to external stakeholders. We consider how the focal aspects change the traditional tasks from project to program management (Smyth 2009). Table 4.2 highlights required modifications going from projects to programs based on the recommendations of Thiry (2002) and Maylor et al. (2006).

From Integrated Management to Decision Management

Within projects, integration management refers to a series of solutions and techniques to ensure all the activities within the project are coordinated and effectively integrated into the final deliverable. The task of project managers is to achieve integration with high levels of performance, with clearly defined outputs, and under resource limitations. Development and implementation of project management are based on a project plan with predefined strategies and monitoring processes, where everything is managed to go as planned.

Programs are less predictable and involve more stakeholders and more intermediate decision making to be more responsive to actual conditions. Program managers need to ensure that programs are well planned, but at the same time need to be open to the possibility of change to achieve ultimate benefits. Establishing a decision process that continually evaluates opportunities to improve delivered benefits to meet strategic goals best serves the nature of programs. Transformation of an organization cannot be restricted to a rigid goal set but must allow continuous adjustment.

From Scope Management to Stakeholder Value Management

Before the implementation of a project, an organization defines project scope, schedule, and budget to the satisfaction of a primary sponsor or stakeholder. The plans and expectations represent an agreement with stakeholders on the deliverable. Thus, managing toward the specific contract requires the accomplishment of scope to satisfy the intended users of the output according to the budget and schedule. However, programs create value for multiple stakeholders in the organization. Therefore, program management requires value management to identify the needs and expectations of stakeholders (often identified through tools such as Strategy Maps or Balanced Scorecards). Expectations must be reduced to quantitative measures to mitigate the ambiguity of programs. The projects within a program must be prioritized based on viability and contribution to stated values. Value management is a way to handle sudden change and is a learning-based framework for stakeholder management, where needs are analyzed, a vision is established, a consensus is reached on a target, and benefits or changes identified.

Program managers must play a leading role and be able to deal with influence, power, and motivation, especially in the setting of mature organizations where program managers may be the initiators or sponsors of a program. Program management is not simply a series of decisions as to whether or not a project is included within a program, but rather considers the needs and expectations of stakeholders for a continuously evolving and systematic perspective to develop and revise a plan that can realize expected benefits for an organization.

From Time Management to Pace Management

Projects have clear start and end dates, with task durations and critical path control being the two most important elements of time management. Project managers usually break a project into many smaller activities and then conduct time and cost assessments to identify interdependencies before establishing a project schedule that can accurately predict the duration of the project, as well as manage the status of each activity.

Programs have more ambiguous start and end dates and are composed of many interrelated projects meant to achieve specific tasks. Environmental changes are continually incorporated into a program. Therefore, program managers need to control the overall pace of the projects and benefits realization of the deliverables. Effective tools may be Benefit Maps and Dependency Networks that clarify relationships between benefits and projects as well as project dependencies. "Pace" includes the prioritization of activities based on dependencies and benefits, interests, cash inflows, rollout plans, and stakeholder relationships. Priority management focuses on the realization of benefits that enable programs to contribute to the overall value of organizations and reduce the unpredictability derived from the pursuit of short-term economic benefits.

From Cost Management to Overall Resource Management

Project cost management includes cost assessments, budgeting, and cost control, making it possible for projects to complete within approved budgets. However, program budgeting includes costs of supporting activities and investment in supporting structures. Program managers participate in setting project budgets but often need to adjust periodically to allow programs to achieve organizational goals successfully. The program retains control over resource allocation to the individual projects, including shared resources that demand constant coordination. Additionally, as budget management is closely related to suppliers and customers, program managers should devote themselves to building long-term and stable relationships with sources of resources as well as sources of additional funding. Program budgets focus on the realization of future financial and nonfinancial benefits, encompassing a wide scope of resources rather than pure monetary benefits, while cost management still continually reviews preset benchmarks to avoid disparities.

From Quality Management to Benefit Management

Quality is one of the key success factors of projects, and quality management focuses on both the processes and the final outputs, to encompass all activities involved in meeting customer demands. However, in programs, benefits are seen as key success factors. As demand and expectations are closely linked, quality management in programs focuses on the achievement of strategic goals, which may change over time.

Benefits are not only the ultimate goal of programs but also a means of monitoring implementation effectiveness. Program managers should be committed to the pursuit of benefits, rather than focusing on new products or development of production technology, as these are merely processes for reaching final benefits. Benefits are directly related to strategic goals, but contributions cannot be fully assessed until program outputs are put into operation or are made available on the market. Therefore, program managers need to look at benefits over the entire life of a program to determine how this contributes to overall strategic goals.

Elevating Stakeholder Management

In projects, stakeholder management is primarily a function of information exchange regarding requirements determination of the output, resource acquisition, and progress reporting. Stakeholder management in programs is an interactive relationship that encompasses stakeholder contributions to a program and selection of team members. Programs have a larger range of stakeholders than projects to perform many of the main functions of knowledge and resource acquisition, but further to external groups that influence both goals and means.

Additionally, since many program stakeholders often have greater formal authority than program managers, program managers need to influence and convince stakeholders to pursue overall interests. The politics are magnified. The need to promote the program and its benefits increase dramatically. The reach both internal to the organization and outside the organization is broader and more complex. Thus, program managers must understand the positions and attitudes of numerous stakeholders, how stakeholders exert influence, and the sources of stakeholder authority. Mature organizations will demonstrate strong stakeholder management capabilities and develop corresponding systems for stakeholder assistance.

From Communication Management to Marketing Management

In projects, communication management is a process where communication paths, frequency, and causes ensure collection, storage, and dissemination of relevant information. However, when a project is part of a program, the communication between projects and organizations or programs need to be more specific. Therefore, communication planning is part of the initial project proposal rather than a part of the project itself.

In programs, the term marketing refers to more than just advertising, and is rather a core element of value creation that includes concepts of value identification, resource provisioning, and communication. Good marketing integrates strategy and is one of the key success factors of programs as it can facilitate the management and participation of stakeholders. Marketing management is an interactive communication system applied to obtain the support of stakeholders and meet their specific needs with targeted benefits. Identification of benefits, as well as techniques for benefits realization and effectiveness of outcomes, maintains motivation for stakeholder cooperation and at the same time facilitates rapid decision making.

From Risk Management to Uncertainty Management

Although the goal of risk management is to reduce the probability and impact of negative events on projects, this often sets a constraint on project activities. Uncertainty management provides a more comprehensive perspective, taking into account potential threats and opportunities and the overall organizational viewpoint when considering risks and their relevant impact. Project risk management relies purely on data analytics and rational decision making, but complex projects and programs involve many factors and changing circumstances, and therefore is difficult to predict risks and mitigations based on historical data. Therefore, uncertainty management helps to avoid deviations from the ultimate goals of the organization. Uncertainty in programs is often managed through iterative cycles of defining goals for early projects, refining them for new projects based on monitoring the environment, and launching new projects when a specific need can be addressed by the deliverable of a new project.

From Procurement Management to Partner Relations and Value Chain Management

In projects, supplier partnerships are often based on short-term contracts. In programs, contractors, such as consultants and suppliers, are not responsible for a limited material or task, but rather are involved with multiple projects and longer term contracts, often on-demand. Authority is transferred from the person responsible for the contract (the program manager) to the organizational level, which requires program managers to negotiate with the most influential stakeholders. Maintaining a long-term partnership is highly important.

A program can be thought of in terms of a value chain that includes several different actors to generate internal and external outcomes, as shown in Figure 4.3. Learning enables customer needs to be accurately delivered to suppliers, while the performance of the suppliers generates value that feeds back through the project to reach the final customer

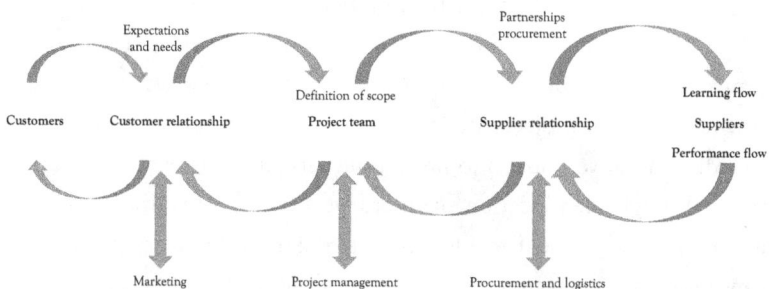

Figure 4.3 The value chain of programs requiring external suppliers

(internal or external). Each stage inward reveals additional information about the value expectations of the customer. Each step out transforms supplier output into a valued facet of the final program benefits. Organizations prefer durable partner management at the supplier interface rather than piecemeal procurement management when acquiring external resources.

Vision-Led and Emergent Programs

Vision-led programs are the more mature type of program and are based on strategic goals. Program complexities and ambiguities require a great deal of flexibility in the initial stage, and visions should be clearly stated before launch. A vision-driven approach is based on clear-cut goals, but program sponsors may still override implementation plans or make major changes during the formulation stage. Contributions of a program are not judged in a purely economic fashion, but rather by a wider range of organizational benefits.

The success of a vision-led program depends on the adoption of an organic approach that focuses on innovation, flexible changes, and employee empowerment rather than a fragmented, control-oriented, mechanistic approach. Organizations that pursue risk minimization rather than maximization of opportunities find further obstacles to implementation. The primary goal for vision-led program managers is to create a business plan to clarify the program vision and organize to prepare for change. While environmental changes may influence different aspects and require the cooperation of all units, stakeholder management can help all managers to achieve individual and organizational goals simultaneously.

Emergent programs form because potential sponsors find that new projects or activities could be more effective when integrated with other projects having similar goals and share extensive resources. In emergent programs, several projects are included, and there is a common strategy to reduce negative impacts to project outputs and to maximize effectiveness. Through identification of interdependencies, organizational goals are more closely linked to business interests rather than mere outputs. Once program management takes effect all projects will be individually reviewed, and redundancies or ineffective contributors to the overall program are terminated, delayed, or distributed to other programs, or new projects may come into effect as a result.

For emergent programs, it is necessary to identify a clear vision and stakeholder needs as early as possible to quickly find projects and activities that will ensure the success of the program and to eliminate those who distract from success. Evaluative techniques used in the selection of projects by the organization must apply, perhaps in an expedited fashion. In practice, many programs are categorized as emergent programs, where projects are mostly initialized according to the needs of each business unit. During budget reviews, these projects are linked to organizational strategic goals, budgets are adjusted, and these autonomous projects are seldom considered from a program perspective.

Key Factors of Program Management

The first key factor of program management is decision making. In less complex environments, decision makers usually make immediate decisions based on established guidelines rooted in rationality or expertise. In highly complex but slowly changing environments, for example, in large-scale government infrastructure projects, we often make collaborative decisions, which is to say, we focus on team participation and collective wisdom. However, these two decision-making situations do not apply to highly complex and rapidly changing environments such as those faced by program managers, where the main concern is a clarification of management implications for the entire project collection in dynamic environments (Pellegrinelli et al. 2015; Näsänen and Vanharanta 2016).

Since the nature of program management includes transformation, and the program management team is the implementer of transformation, the program team conforms decisions to three principles:

1. Value creation requires transformation. Decisions require an understanding of the significance and necessity of the proposed transformation. Program team members and key stakeholders must reach a consensus on any value proposal and understand the consequences of any transformation as well as the consequences of failing to transform. As transformation involves complex environments and mul-

tiple stakeholders, there is inherent ambiguity. Unlike uncertainty, ambiguity can be resolved through good management. Management of ambiguity requires a common understanding of the reasons, expectations, and consequences behind any values, goals, or activities. Leadership must ensure that stakeholders first understand the potential impacts of change and reach a consensus on expected benefits.

2. Achieving a transformation requires the allocation of limited resources and the application of transformational processes. Ambiguity and uncertainty need to be translated into resources and action. For these decisions, traditional project management tools and techniques may prove valid. Project management can reduce the uncertainty of tasks, while program management defines and maintains a vision that allows organizations to adapt to constantly changing environments.

3. Realizing benefits requires integration of the transformation into the organization to achieve a steady state. When outputs are internalized by an organization, the program management team must establish coordination and good communication with the operational team to determine the best approaches to instill the relevant changes as new capabilities.

Typical decision-making techniques for program management combine learning (value management) and performance (project management). Through the integration of learning and performance-based approaches associated with decision-making and implementation processes, we derive a decision-making framework, as shown in Figure 4.4. This framework is divided into two parts, with one part being the decision-making process, where requirements, problems, and feasible solutions are identified through learning and presented for evaluation and selection. The second part is the implementation of decisions, including planning and execution of selected projects. Results must be assessed and lead to decisions of adjustments to the program.

The second key element of program management is governance. Governance clarifies and maintains project progress through the adoption of appropriate organizational forms for achieving established goals and benefits. Compared with traditional governance models focused on the pursuit of short-term financial benefits from the perspective of shareholders,

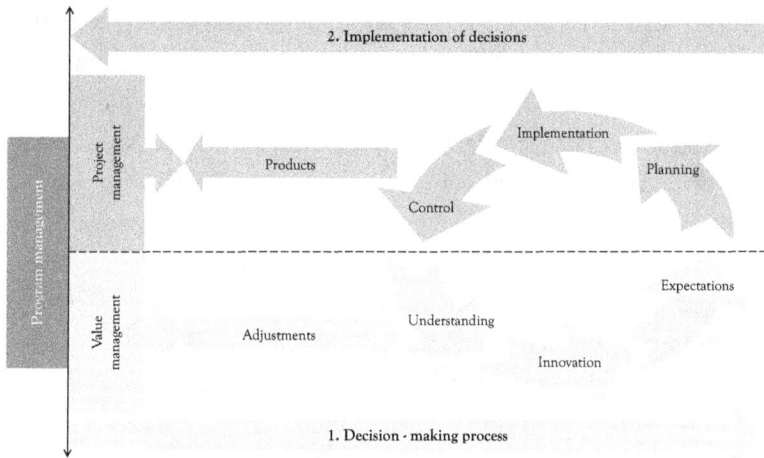

Figure 4.4 Decision-making process of program management

governance of program management focuses on long-term organizational performance from a collective stakeholder perspective. De Wit and Meyer (2002) defined the three main functions of governance as:

- Structure: organizational structures that impact and control tasks.
- Implementation: used to establish strategy processes to enhance future performance.
- Consistency: ensuring consistency between existing tasks and strategies within a company.

Program governance relies on business strategies, complexities, and stakeholder needs. Visions and goals of program management are established, and then appropriate organizational structures adopted and resources allocated to achieve the vision. One of the key elements of program governance is the establishment of a monitoring system to ensure the right decisions are made, and projects are rescheduled when necessary.

The third key element of program management is stakeholder management. Stakeholders are individuals or organizations that may be affected positively or negatively by programs, or who may have an impact on the outcomes of programs. Management requires analysis, influence, and monitoring of different stakeholders and their needs, including identification of stakeholders, categorization of stakeholders, recording and understanding stakeholder needs and expectations, assessment of expectations, coordination between different stakeholders, finding consensus based on value targets, and implementation of real-time reviews.

The fourth key element of program management is benefits management. Benefits are tangible results that meet stakeholder requirements. Benefits management supplements stakeholder management; identification and realization of important benefits can only be ensured through effective management of stakeholders (Pellegrinelli et al. 2007). Processes include identifying and selecting key benefits, assessing returns, and achieving returns during the implementation.

Program Management Processes: A Life Cycle Perspective

Although there is no standardized management framework or technique for program management, the process of program management follows a specific life cycle where stages follow a pattern of continued repetition individually or in combination rather than a traditional linear process. Research indicates that the life cycle of a program divides into the six stages shown in Figure 4.5, where a formulation stage begins the process with the inception of program goals to meet specific organizational strategies, either existing, revised or new. In this stage, results of a stakeholder analysis are the basis for defining expected benefits of a program and ensure that all stakeholders agree on the goals of the program.

The development stage considers the complicated task of crafting an initial implementation plan based on the requirements of the stakeholders' goals. Key success factors are established, and initial business plans with functional blueprints for both program management and project management are presented.

The organizational stage sets up the project structure and resources to move the organization toward the strategies. In this stage, specific business actions of the program are debated, and the main goal is to organize project collections to achieve program goals through discussion of organizational structures, revenue realization plans, operational processes, and technical blueprints.

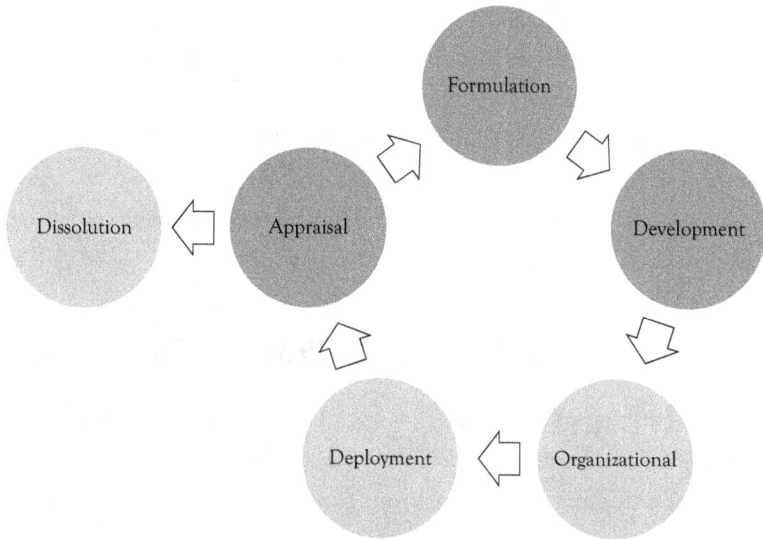

Figure 4.5 The life cycle of a program

Deployment is the phased implementation of the program deliverables. This phase focuses on delivering expected benefits of a program through the development of synergies formed through the management of stakeholders, key project initiatives, activities, and outcomes. Specific activities include management of value chains (stakeholders, management teams, resource priorities, dependencies, risks, and transformations), management of transformation activities, and integration of new capabilities. This stage is often implemented in a looped rather than a linear pattern.

An appraisal is an evaluation of the benefits realized, or not, after deployment. This phase emphases repeated, real-time evaluation of results to determine whether programs have achieved expected profit targets, upon which the program manager should decide whether the program should be continued, redeployed, or immediately terminated. Knowledge management in the appraisal stage is an important element as program management runs in cycles, so the knowledge acquired within one cycle can often be applied to the next cycle, embodying continued learning in program management (Pollack 2012). A decision is made based on the appraisal of whether the program has reached the final goals or further actions and projects are required—leading into a new iteration starting with the formulation.

Dissolution is the end of the program's life where transformations are completed to a level of satisfaction and benefits captured, allowing reallocation of dedicated resources and a final evaluation of the products and processes of the program in its entirety. Programs may extend over extremely long time horizons, but must have a terminal goal to enable dissolution decisions. This stage also focuses on the transfer of knowledge captured throughout, particularly from the assessment.

Limitations and Challenges of Program Management

At the beginning of this chapter, we pointed out that program management requires a completely new set of management concepts and cultures that differ from traditional project management. As a result, deeply engrained management concepts adopted by project managers are the biggest obstacle to successful program management. Managers continue to apply traditional concepts of project management such as cost savings, risk reductions, and the timely achievement of tasks, and continue to adhere to standardized project management processes and rigid project management frameworks. Changing these existing conceptual frameworks will prove to be a big managerial challenge.

One aspect of most difficulty is that traditional project managers are faced with clear goals and task-specific projects, and adhere to a set of standardized management practices to ensure timely delivery of the final product or services. However, when managing programs where end results may be ambiguous in the initial stages and management objectives may change over time, project managers may find that they are "stretched," as they do not have the appropriate managerial capabilities. Unlike traditional project management, program management requires managers to have a tolerance for uncertainty and ambiguity. Managers who lack this basic characteristic may find difficulties in managing programs.

Program management focuses on sets of projects that still target a common goal set. A program lacks the scope required for a complete organizational overhaul. For example, we mentioned that a program might consider a transformation to penetrate new markets, to implement new quality control systems at multiple levels in the organization, to alter a corporate culture to become more consumer oriented, or adjust to new legislation or social expectations. However, what if one wanted to accomplish all of these transformations? Program management practices could not handle such a variety of objectives. For such situations, we must advance another step and consider the practice of project portfolio management.

Discussion Questions

1. If a program seems perpetual, what might you do to realize earlier dissolution?
2. Describe how development of a new product might be a project but development of a new product line might be implemented as a program.
3. What employment practices might you implement during a program of long duration to ensure availability of talented project managers?
4. What benefits can you identify for a program to reduce employee turnover? Can you break those benefits into deliverables for multiple projects?
5. In your organization, who would you include in the decision to dissolve a program?

References

Chang, J.Y.T., J.J. Jiang, G. Klein., and T.G. Eric. Wang. 2014. "Do Too Many Goals Impede a Program? A Case Study of Enterprise System Implementation with Multiple Interdependent Projects." *Information and Management* 51, no. 4, 465–478. doi: 10.1016/j.im.2014.03.004

Dutton, C., N. Turner, and L. Lee-Kelley. 2014. "Learning in a Program Context: An Exploratory Investigation of Drivers and Constraints." *International Journal of Project Management* 32, no. 5, 747–758. doi: 10.1016/j.ijproman.2014.02.003

Ferns, D.C. 1991. "Developments in Programme Management." *International Journal of Project Management* 9, no. 3, 148–156. doi: 10.1016/0263-7863(91)90039-X

Jiang, J.J., J.Y. Chang, H.G. Chen, E.T. Wang, and G. Klein. 2014. "Achieving IT Program Goals with Integrative Conflict Management." *Journal of Management Information Systems* 31, no. 1, 79–106. doi: 10.2753/MIS0742-1222310104

Martinsuo, M., and P. Hoverfält. 2018. "Change Program Management: Toward a Capability for Managing Value-Oriented, Integrated Multi-Project Change in its Context." *International Journal of Project Management* 36, no. 1, pp. 134–146. doi: 10.1016/j.ijproman.2017.04.018

Maylor, H., T. Brady, T. Cooke-Davies, and D. Hodgson. 2006. "From Projectification to Programmification." *International Journal of Project Management* 24, no. 8, 663–674. doi: 10.1016/j.ijproman.2006.09.014

Näsänen, J., and O. Vanharanta. 2016. "Program Group's Discursive Construction of Context: A Means to Legitimize Buck-Passing." *International Journal of Project Management* 34, no. 8, 1672–1686. doi: 10.1016/ j.ijproman.2016.09.008

OGC. 2011. *Managing Successful Programmes*, 3rd ed. Norwich, U.K: Office of Government Commerce.

Pellegrinelli, S., D. Partington, C. Hemingway, and M. Shah. 2007. "The Importance of Context in Program Management: An Empirical Review of Program Practices." *International Journal of Project Management* 25, no. 1, 41–55. doi: 10.1016/j.ijproman.2006.06.002

Pellegrinelli, S., Ruth Murray-Webster, and Neil Turner. 2015. "Facilitating Organizational Ambidexterity through the Complementary Use of Projects and Programs." *International Journal of Project Management* 33, no. 1, 153–164. doi: 10.1016/j.ijproman.2014.04.008

Pellegrinelli, S. 2011. "What's in a Name: Project or Program?" *International Journal of Project Management* 29, no. 2, 232–240. doi: 10.1016/ j.ijproman.2010.02.009

Pich, M.T. C.H. Loch, and A. De Meyer. 2002. "On Uncertainty, Ambiguity, and Complexity in Project Management." *Management Science* 48, no. 8, 1008–1023. doi: 10.1287/mnsc.48.8.1008.163

PMI Standard Committee. 2017. *The Standard for Program Management*, 4th ed. Newton Square, PMI.

Pollack, J. 2012. "Transferring Knowledge About Knowledge Management: Implementation of a Complex Organizational Change Program." *International Journal of Project Management* 30, no. 8, 877–886. doi: 10.1016/j.ijproman.2012.04.001

Smyth, H.J. 2009. "Projects and Programs: Diversity of Management, Diversity of Aims, and Interests." *International Journal of Project Management* 27, no. 2, 97–100. doi: 10.1016/j.ijproman.2008.11.001

Thiry, M. 2002. "Combining Value and Project Management into an Effective Program Management Model." *International Journal of Project Management* 20, no. 3, 221–227. doi: 10.1016/S0263-7863(01)00072-2

Thiry, M. 2004. "For DAD: A Program Management Life-Cycle Process." *International Journal of Project Management* 22, no. 3, 245–252. doi: 10.1016/S0263-7863(03)00064-4

Thiry, M. 2010. *Program Management*. Gower.

CHAPTER 5

Project Portfolio Management

- Without project portfolio management, there can be no realization of organizational strategy.
- Implementation of poorly chosen projects, even when executed flawlessly, is nonsensical.
- Correct project and program collections inevitably represent the motives, direction, and progress of an organization.
- Project portfolio management stems from limited organization resources and organizational strategic goals, where the right projects ensure ultimate success.

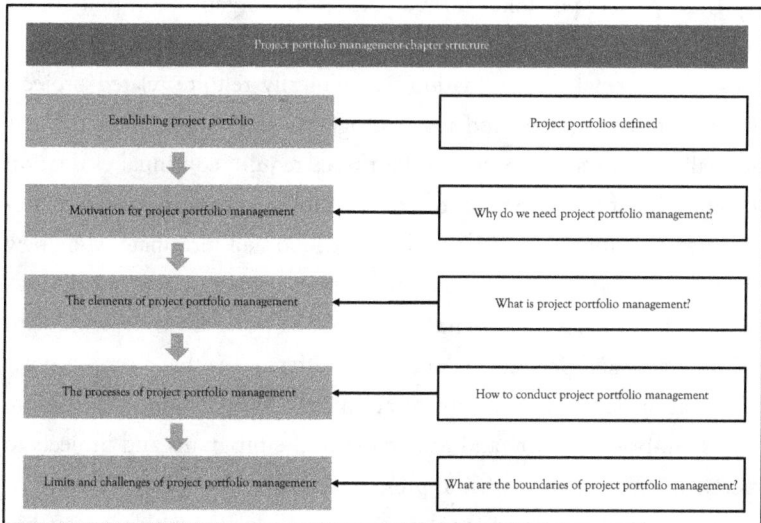

Project portfolio management chapter structure

Establishing project portfolio	Project portfolios defined
Motivation for project portfolio management	Why do we need project portfolio management?
The elements of project portfolio management	What is project portfolio management?
The processes of project portfolio management	How to conduct project portfolio management
Limits and challenges of project portfolio management	What are the boundaries of project portfolio management?

Chapter Structure

What is a Project Portfolio?

As it seems with every human endeavor, once we get traction on a particular problem, we begin to tackle the next level of difficulty. We still struggle with programs and even projects that go beyond the more simplistic. However, projects only view short-term gain from very specific deliverables. Programs address some of that concern by considering long-term, but narrow, strategic initiatives. The next level of difficulty we must tackle is that of having an entire collection of projects and programs dedicated to transitioning the organization to a future vision. For that, we turn to the management of projects and programs as portfolios.

A project portfolio is a specific collection of programs and projects dedicated to the achievement of strategic goals for an organization, independent divisions within an organization, or a substantial strategic initiative within the organization or division that requires multiple programs or projects. Thus, portfolios also have a purpose defined by time, albeit a typically long horizon. Project portfolios open at the start of any new initiative that spans multiple units within an organization or includes major strategic pursuits. Project portfolios close when completing the intended strategic objectives, when merged with other portfolios, or when the pursuit is no longer deemed worthwhile for the continued existence of the organization.

Thus, project portfolios form a place in the organization that attend unique divisions or strategies with a collection of programs and projects. An organizational transformation will typically require related projects that fall into programs, and many programs and independent projects that fall into a specific portfolio. Portfolios require continual evaluation to determine if the current set of projects and programs match the strategic intent. Elements within a project portfolio will terminate while new projects or programs may enter. Thus, just as a program is dynamic concerning the projects in a program collection, a portfolio is dynamic with the programs and projects included. The difference is that a project portfolio is at the level where an organization conducts decisions of inclusion, exclusion, prioritization, and resourcing of the programs and projects to meet strategic initiatives while programs are at lower levels directed at achieving specific benefits for the organization in line with strategy, but not typically moving the strategy of the organization (Pendharkar 2014).

The Motivation for Project Portfolio Management

Traditional project management is concerned with using limited resources to accomplish well-defined project goals and to deliver products within a limited period of time. In other words, traditional project management is concerned with the specifics of implementing a project. At the organizational level, a more fundamental question that needs exploration is: Why should the organization develop projects (or project collections)? Furthermore, why did the organization choose to run projects A and C rather than project B? Why was project A rather than project C started first? The need to place projects, even when every project is a valuable pursuit, through a selection and prioritization process is prominent in an organization.

Building Optimal Project Portfolios Under Limited Resources

The resources (human resources, material inputs, facility space, and financial resources) of each organization are limited. On the one hand, limited resources force implementation of different projects, but if there is a lack of appropriate evaluation criteria for project selection, project decision making will be subjective and will fail to consider project benefits at the strategic level, thus ignoring longer term benefits. On the other hand, limited resources often result in conflict and dispute among projects as each strives to acquire key resources. Further, redundant projects will be wasting the limited resources of an organization. Thus, if managers fail to view organizations from an overall systemic and strategic perspective or fail to unify resource management and allocation, the result will be a waste of financial and human resources.

Successful Projects May Still Be Strategic Failures

There is no organizational strategy without project portfolio management. Traditional project management facilitates the success of a single project but fails to guarantee the success of the organizational strategy. Projects that are highly feasible and show positive returns may still be abandoned if the strategic goals of the project do not align with organizational strategic goals, because projects or project collections must be in line with organizational motives, directions, and progress. As an extreme example, even if Starbucks found positive returns on drilling for oil in Seattle, it could not invest without a major transformation of corporate strategy. A lack of strategic direction might bring short-term benefits, but the success of projects that do not match organizational strategy is not conducive to long-term sustainability.

Inability to Respond to Strategic Changes

Lack of coordination among different projects makes it difficult to respond to strategic changes within an organization or move toward an intended transformation. Changes in the external and internal environment require organizations to adjust their strategies and goals. The strategic change affects many projects, communication between projects (e.g., stakeholders may be required to justify portfolio adjustments), and risk management. Without unified management for strategic change, organizations will fail to respond in a timely and effective manner to strategic transformations, which may lead to strategic failures.

The limitations of traditional single project management frameworks do not allow a response to the aforementioned concerns. Effective project portfolio management overcomes the limitations of traditional project management discussed earlier and adopts a unified approach in the management of strategic goals by evaluating, selecting, and prioritizing projects and programs. Project portfolio management not only admits that organizations face challenges in expanding traditional project management to more expansive circumstances but also provides five key outcomes for an organization (PMI 2017).

1. Project portfolios must organize strategy, resources, risk constraints, future returns, and stakeholder expectations by adjusting, authorizing, and controlling portfolio elements to ensure that project portfolio end goals are in line with current organizational strategy.
2. The project portfolio charter provides a formal structure indicating when and where managers have the authority to allocate resources between portfolios, programs, and projects.
3. The project portfolio management plan describes the identification, authorization, implementation, prioritization, balance, manage-

ment, and reporting of project portfolios, programs, projects, and operational tasks to achieve strategic goals.

4. Project portfolio plans provide strategic guidance by showing chronological implementations and interdependencies among various projects that form that basis of portfolio management.

5. There are not necessarily dependencies or direct relationships between the elements in a project portfolio, but each element must be quantifiable; in other words, measurable, ratable, and sortable.

The Management Of Project Portfolios

Project portfolio management utilizes evaluations of each proposed project or program and optimization of project and program combinations to ensure that the portfolios conform to organizational strategic goals and maximize business benefits.

Going Beyond Projects and Programs

Rather than simply managing multiple projects, project portfolio management goes beyond the boundaries of traditional project management by bridging the gap between projects and organizational strategies, thus integrating project implementation with business strategy. Collaborative management of one or more projects to achieve organizational strategic goals includes assessment, selection, prioritization, and allocation of limited internal resources for use in organizational processes that best enable fit organizational visions, missions, and values (Unger et al. 2012). Project portfolio management generates valuable information to support or adjust organizational strategy and investment decisions (Pendharkar 2014).

We differentiate certain traits between traditional project management and project portfolio management in Table 5.1. Traditional project management is a bottom-up, "how to implement projects" approach where the management activities ensure effective project management, timely delivery, and adherence to cost and quality requirements. This type of management focuses primarily on management and implementation of individual projects or project collections.

Table 5.1 Comparison of management traits

	Project portfolio management	**Traditional project management**
Management techniques	Top-down	Bottom-up
Management scope	All projects in a portfolio	Single projects or project groups
Management cycles	Long term, lasting as long as there are projects within the bounds of intent	Short term, from initiation to termination of projects
Main managers	Upper level managers	Project managers
Major stakeholders	Business executives/financial managers/stockholders	Project sponsors/project managers/customers

Project portfolio management, on the other hand, is a top-down, "what projects and programs to implement" approach that integrates organizational strategy and balances multiple projects by focusing on those that generate the most value. Traditional project management collects data from the lower levels of projects and sends these to the upper levels for project management. This collection often fails to capture deviations from strategic goals promptly. Project portfolio management, however, prioritizes strategic objectives and selects the best projects and programs to ensure effective implementation within resource constraints. The selection process defines the scope of the portfolio. The cycle is a repetitive process that continues until satisfaction or abandonment of the intended strategic objective. Decisions about inclusion and direction fall under the responsibilities of upper management or even a team of executives. The level of key stakeholders raises to the upper levels of management and ownership.

The Elements of Project Portfolio Management

Table 5.2 shows how the aspects evolve from projects to programs, and to portfolios, and provides a clear picture as to why management

Table 5.2 Focal aspects of project, program, and project portfolio management

Aspect	Projects	Programs	Portfolios
Targeted Deliverable	Clear, defined deliverable	Defined business benefits	Organizational goals
Performance Criteria	Cost, time, scope, quality	Attainment of benefits	Ongoing organizational performance
Change Flexibility	Avoid change	Capitalize on change	Invest according to the strategic direction
Interaction	Related to tasks, product delivery	Related to pacing and coordination of projects, delivery of benefits	Resource management, ownership value
Control	Compare actuals to schedules, budgets, and specifications	Compare delivered benefits to expectations, continual assessment of projects	Compare the total value with performance indicators
Task Orientation	Define and complete work, manage teams and risks	Market the program, monitor the environment	Prioritize projects and programs, assess and reassess the value

techniques for projects do not translate to higher levels. Projects exist in a well-defined world, even in the face of complexity, where deliverables are oriented to the operational. Programs aim to a higher level of contribution, considering multiple deliverables coordinated to achieve a particular benefit. Project portfolios pursue the organizational vision by supporting organizational strategies and goals. Performance considerations vary from specific items of budget, scope, and schedule in projects, to the attainment of the desired benefit in programs, to the overall performance of meeting strategic targets in project portfolios. In projects, change is controlled. In programs, identified change serves to adjust the direction taken by the project collection. Change requires adjustment of those projects under the control of the program. Change at the portfolio level requires an assessment of strategic direction, perhaps resulting in required transformation.

Interactions in the management of project portfolios involve coordination processes to facilitate the smooth progress of an organization toward strategic goals. Direct communication of resource allocations, project and program priorities, and other implementation concerns flow between lower management levels and those involved with managing the portfolio. There may be more than one project portfolio within an organization, and therefore it is necessary to implement an organizationwide team that enjoys the support of all levels of management when pushing requirements and allocations to lower levels. Communication management first identifies a large number of stakeholders performing basic tasks, collaborating third parties, and investors. Though details may be less, the breadth of information required for project portfolio management surpasses that of information communicated at project and program levels, and therefore project portfolio managers have a wider range of stakeholders.

Control requires confirmation that tasks are consistent with established plans and tasks fall within the governing rules of the organization. Thus, the core tasks of control require a prior formulation of plans, a thorough risk assessment, and a governance structure to monitor progress and change. Plans include aspects of strategic direction, metrics applied in the selection of projects or programs, communication paths, risk assessment and mitigation, and a roadmap of implementation that highlights the prioritization and resourcing of the projects and programs in the portfolio (Too and Weaver 2014).

Controlling risk requires a structured process for evaluating and analyzing portfolio risks to take advantage of potential opportunities that may reduce the number of events, activities, or circumstances that impact negatively on project portfolios. When interdependencies are present between high priority elements, the costs of element failure become high since the risks and completion of any one component may affect the risks and completion of another component (Paquin et al. 2016). An organization must further monitor all components for variations of progress or failure to meet projections of performance metrics. Sources of variation include opportunities and threats due to changes in the environment, poor planning, interdependencies among the projects and programs, new investors, strategic redirection, and failure of an element.

Task orientation is reliant on organizational structures. The organization may employ a portfolio management team or a formal portfolio office. Core responsibilities of the portfolio management team or office include integrated management and coordination of project portfolios. The scope of responsibility ranges from general support of project portfolios to management of specific portfolios. Specific tasks of the portfolio management office differ according to the different needs of an organization and its stakeholders, but may include (PMI 2017; Unger, Gemunden, and Aubry 2012):

- Management of portfolio components; support for component proposals and evaluations; prioritization and authorization; resource allocation to ensure consistency with organizational strategies and goals.
- Development and maintenance of project portfolios, project collections, and project frameworks and techniques.
- Provision of information and benchmarking reports (of costs, deficiencies, and resources) during the portfolio governance processes.
- Negotiation between portfolios and allocation of resources between different project portfolios.
- Identification of risks and establishment of risk management strategies, as well as communication of risks and issues relating to portfolio components.
- Coordination of communication between project portfolio components.
- Development and improvement of templates and checklists.
- Monitoring of adherence to policy.
- Provision of knowledge management including compilations of past experiences.
- Development and implementation of portfolio management techniques, tools, and the training and counseling of technical personnel.

Portfolio managers are responsible for executing portfolio management processes. Portfolio managers collect performance and progress information of portfolio components and deliver these to portfolio governance authorities to confirm that they align with overall strategic goals, and may provide advice and comments as appropriate to ensure adherence to project portfolio management processes and schedules (Jonas 2010). Portfolio managers dictate information from portfolio elements (projects and project collections, ongoing operations from completed projects and programs) and serve as a bridge between lower managers and project portfolio stakeholders.

Processes Of Project Portfolio Management

A Framework for Project Portfolio Management

Structural implementation of project portfolio management often increases the long-term value of business units and organizations. A study of previous research on project portfolio management and standards of the Project Management Institute yields the framework of project portfolio management shown in Figure 5.1.

The main purpose of strategic positioning is to determine whether project goals are consistent with the strategic direction of an organization, to delineate the boundaries of the portfolio in terms of a particular strategy and provide a guiding vision. Portfolio visions should be in line with organizational visions, strategies, and goals, as portfolio visions

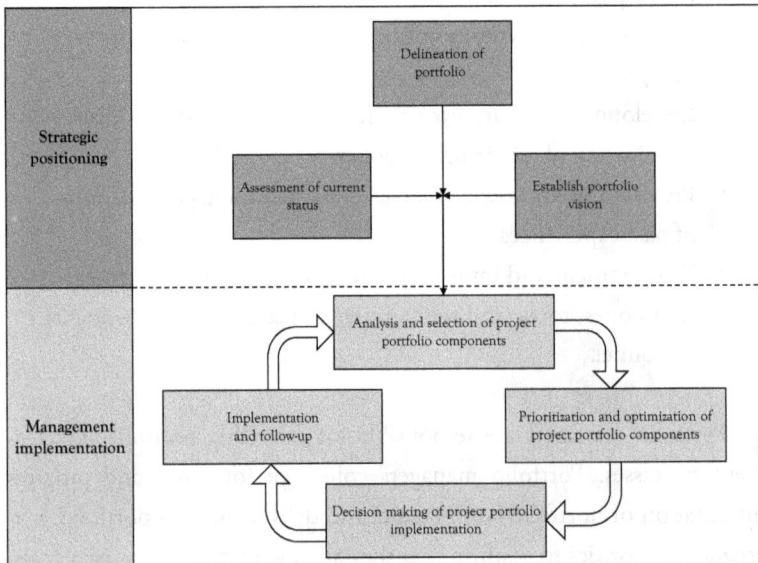

Figure 5.1 Framework of project portfolio management

help to define the direction of the portfolio and enable the monitoring of progress. Overall, the main essence of this preimplementation is to break down the strategic goals of an organization and classify projects according to strategic objectives, such that the strategic goals of projects align with those of the organization, thus providing a foundation for resource allocation (Ghapanchi et al. 2012, p. 798). To do this, it is necessary to conduct a comparative analysis of ongoing project portfolio statuses and project portfolio plans.

Assessment of current portfolio statuses and related processes helps managers conduct a gap analysis to see which processes are already in place and what processes, portfolios, or cultural traits may need implementation or become obstacles. The assessment may facilitate plan establishment or serve as formal confirmation of portfolio functions. Once a full understanding is gained of all components, the analyses establish an information and resource database that serves in decisions regarding any current or proposed element in the portfolio (Unger et al. 2012, p. 682). Completion of strategic positioning leads to consider implementation management.

By its nature, the implementation of a project portfolio is cyclical. Over the long course of a portfolio's life, an organization continually seeks new opportunities that may dictate new programs or projects to be added to the portfolio. If the evaluation of a particular initiative proves fruitful, then a reshuffling of the priorities within the portfolio is warranted. Approvals follow that launch the need for assignment of resources and responsibilities to the lower levels of program and project managers. The implementation of these elements then begins, but is carefully monitored for contribution to the overall portfolio. We first present an overview description of these four general tasks and provide more detail in the following sections.

As stakeholders in the organization generate ideas for new initiatives, each must be analyzed to determine the contribution to the achievement of the strategy. If the analysis indicates the initiative has value, a project or program launches as a new element in the portfolio. This stage is important to the entire project portfolio management process as its core essence is to establish a uniform evaluation of potential elements for organizational portfolios, with benchmarks to measure all project portfolio components regarding resources, progress, costs, risks, and other relevant factors. Finally, portfolio components that do not meet evaluation standards are discarded. Existing elements require periodic evaluation to determine their value in relation to new additions.

The main purpose of prioritization and optimization of project portfolio elements is to provide a plan that sets up the implementation of the individual elements in a feasible fashion according to resource constraints, such as cash flows, and gain the highest benefits earlier in the implementation of the entire collection. Without resource limitations, all projects with a positive benefit would be selected and scheduled to begin immediately. Thus, optimization is highly constrained by resources and other initiatives in the organization. This stage sets out the roadmap followed by lower implementation levels (programs and projects), but without specific resourcing which occurs in the next step.

Once the portfolio is prioritized, decisions about the allocation of resources and timing of element commencement follow. The main purpose of this stage is to make certain that resources will be available as needed or that the output from one element required in a subsequent element is indeed ready for handoff. Decision makers need to combine previous experiences, existing projects in organizations, and specific needs of project users before the implementation of any element. During implementation and follow-up, the organization tracks progress and keeps abreast of status changes of the elements. Further, an organization monitors changes in internal and external environments, evolving strategic goals, and any factor that may significantly alter the mix or priorities of elements in the portfolio.

Implementation of Project Portfolio Management

We now further illustrate project portfolio management implementation with specific implementation procedures, inputs at different levels, and relationships with lower levels in the organization. Implementation begins at the strategic level where management teams must define project portfolios to reflect organizational strategies, reporting structures, regional markets, established policies and practices, and product lines. Figure 5.2 shows the input of organizational fixtures coming in from the

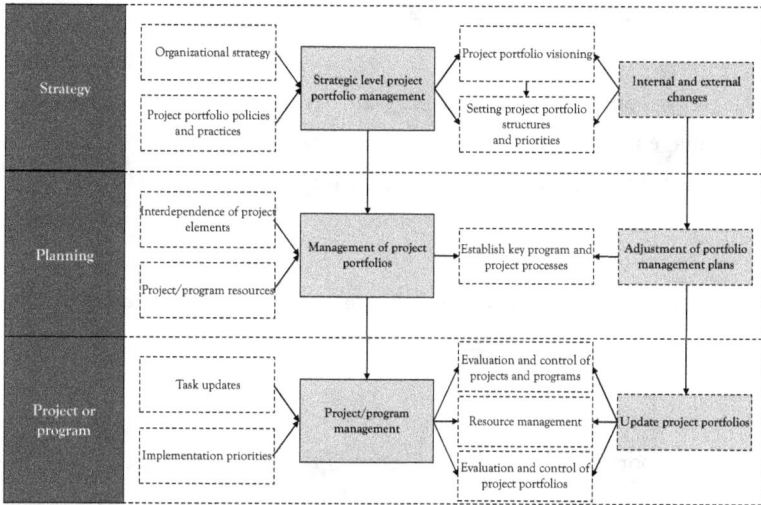

Figure 5.2 The procedures of project portfolio management implementation

left into the management of project portfolios. Procedures at this level include the visioning of the portfolio and the prioritization of those projects and programs selected. These procedures will also require the input of changes to the internal and external environments, shown entering from the right.

Following this, project portfolio management requires projects to be grouped in the planning stage based on resource requirements and interdependency of tasks and local goals, shown entering from the left in the planning level of Figure 5.2. Project portfolio teams and project management teams should work together to compare the objectives and scope of each project within a portfolio, to determine whether there is a direct correlation with organizational strategies and provide direction to the determination of the project solution spaces. Interdependencies must be resolved should there be conflict or adjustments made to portfolio priorities. At this time, any portfolio adjustments made due to corrections or environmental changes must be incorporated into the solution space, as seen entering from the right.

At the project and program level, the implementation teams need to specify implementation methods and processes to match project priorities. Shortage of funds or other key resources must be addressed. Then, projects must be planned, authorized, and managed using management processes based on project groups. At the project level, implementation is managed at the project and program level; however, resources must be managed according to allocations established at higher levels and evaluation of progress conducted according to expectations established at the portfolio level. Feedback from evaluations of the projects and programs permit updates to the project portfolio. One needs to maintain overall progress schedules in accordance with the following three features:

- Establish progress schedules for all projects and programs in the portfolios to reflect priorities of the approved project;
- Utilize communication tools, such as large schedule posters or websites that indicate starts, ends, and important milestones of projects contained in the project portfolios;
- Document and disseminate connections between different projects and interdependencies within project portfolios.

At the same time, managers need to allocate sufficient resources for projects within project portfolios, to achieve the following four purposes:

- Establish comparatively detailed progress and implementation plans for current projects;
- Confirm key resources for project planning and implementation as projects progress;
- Assess the impacts of resource allocation on project progress;
- Revise resource allocations and project status indicators with each portfolio revision.

In short, project portfolio implementation supplements and informs project and program plans, management processes, and governance. Managers can only promote overall project portfolio implementation by clearly defining procedures that then guide the planning and implementation of the programs and projects in the portfolio.

Success Factors of Project Portfolio Management

Successful project portfolio management accomplishes the following in terms of strategy and execution. Firstly, in strategic terms, we need to define clearly the expected goals of projects and then confirm whether resources for execution exceed capacities. Attractiveness and achievability of each potential element determine the priority of project execution. As resistance to change is often encountered in practice, decisive leadership is required for continued execution of project milestones so that managers can detect and correct strategic deviations as soon as possible. In the event of no deviations from strategic goals, achieved project milestones encourage employees to make continuous changes, and eventually form a repeatable process.

Clearly defined goals indicate to project sponsors what the collection of projects is trying to achieve, how generated values will be realized, and whether values are relevant to organizational strategic objectives. Portfolio management facilitates integrated allocation of organizational resources, and therefore, it is not adequate practice to solve current problems and ignore long-term organizational development.

Portfolio scope relates to the capacities of project portfolio management. To achieve strategic objectives, the distribution of organizational resources must be coordinated, and unsuitable projects deleted to avoid failure of strategically aligned projects due to lack of resources. There are two types of projects considered unsuitable for organizations: projects that lack attractiveness and projects with problematic achievability. The former being projects not aligned with organizational strategic objectives, and the latter being projects that are unrealistic or infeasible and, therefore, not worth the investment. If a project is necessary for business operations or in some form valuable, and is also achievable, then the project is worthwhile for the organization to invest resources.

In accordance with the aforementioned principles, projects that are part of the project portfolio should all have clear and definite objectives, and be achievable and worthwhile. However, organizations still need to prioritize different projects based on measurements of attractiveness and achievability . A simple chart, shown in Table 5.3, effectively distinguishes projects. Classify all items in the portfolio into one of the four quadrants. Select those in the highly attractive and highly achievable quadrant first.

Table 5.3 Prioritization of project/program implementation

	High achievability	Low achievability
High attractiveness		
Low attractiveness		

If resources will not allow the selection of all in a category, then add a middle category of "moderate" in each dimension. If further refinement is required, change to a rating of 0 to 10 for attractiveness and achievability. The addition of both scales for each project then serves as a good cut to initiate greater discussion, perhaps along the lines of intangible benefits.

Secure active participation to avoid resistance to changes. Securing participation requires decisive leadership to promote the vision of the portfolio at all levels, open discussions at each level of management, and encourage team strengthening. Feedback to participants focuses attention where needed. Additionally, in our information-rich world, environmental changes occur rapidly, and therefore, it is necessary during the execution of project portfolios to continuously collect information related to observed changes, thus helping to achieve targets. As an example, when projects lose their original values due to environmental changes, the projects should be discarded to avoid excessive waste of resources, or paused and redesigned.

Setting realistic milestones, clearly communicated, provides a metric appreciated by the implementation teams. Overly ambitious milestones reduce people's willingness to work hard and reduce the incentive to conduct an accurate assessment of progress. Even if no deviation occurs, the achievement of milestones encourages employees to accept continuous change. Evaluation of project tasks, actual completion of work packages, and cash flows help to determine whether project costs and progress are in line with original visions.

Limitations and Challenges of Project Portfolio Management

Though project portfolio management has long-reaching consequences for organizations, there are two limitations to consider. The first being that the value of project portfolio components is difficult to measure. To prioritize projects and ensure that projects do not exceed carrying capacities in the future, the portfolio manager must calculate actual values of projects, typically with net present value or return on investment (ROI) analysis, and ensure that benefits are achievable. Note that portfolios imply large commitments over the long term requiring that organizational capacities be large and fiscal analysis institutionalized in a closed loop to assure appropriate feedback and follow-ups.

However, values are not always quantified in cash terms. Parameters used in the computation of the fiscal numbers may vary over the life of the project portfolio. Intangible benefits may prove difficult to include as a determination of value contains subjectivity. For example, if ROI differences between two projects are large, project managers can rely on that data as a basis for decision making. However, when the gap between ROIs is small, managers should not use these numerical data as the sole basis for decision making and rely more on data that may be subjective. When anticipated project values convert readily into cash values, the reliability of these values may be called into question as there are multiple viewpoints for value calculation, and it is difficult to settle on which method of analysis is the most appropriate. To avoid these problems, one might consider numerical range estimates, sensitivity analysis, or investigate the promise of big data.

Estimation procedures arrive at approximations. Three-point estimates are effective devices, similar to the estimation of time in the Program Evaluation and Review Technique of traditional project management that creates a point estimate along with an estimate of variation. Two-point estimation processes provide effective ranges using the subjective responses of experienced managers. Unlike measurements calculated using single digits, measurements taken over an interval can represent risks more adequately. Secondly, sensitivity analysis applies scientific management models to calculate ROIs. Investments are adjusted to calculate increases and decreases in project values per unit of investment, and optimized levels of project outputs and input resources can then be identified, such that we can find the cutoff point for terminating projects due to lack of resources. When organizations collect a large history of portfolio management, emerging techniques in big data analytics may prove valuable tools.

Discussion Questions

1. What evaluation criteria for projects, programs, and portfolio evaluation would you employ? Do these go beyond what your organization currently employs?
2. How would you manage the termination of an ongoing project deemed to have little value in a portfolio?
3. What portfolio management practices reside in your organization? Do they apply to project portfolios?
4. What risks or uncertainties exist at the portfolio level that differ from those at the project or program level?
5. What barriers exist in your organization, or a well-publicized organization, to implementing the three levels of project management (projects, programs, and portfolios)?

References

Ghapanchi, A.H., M. Tavana, M.H. Khakbaz, and G. Low. 2012. "A Methodology for Selecting Portfolios of Projects with Interactions and Under Uncertainty." *International Journal of Project Management* 30, no. 7, 791–803. doi: 10.1016/j.ijproman.2012.01.012

Jonas, D. 2010. "Empowering Project Portfolio Managers: How Management Involvement Impacts Project Portfolio Management Performance." *International Journal of Project Management* 28, no. 8, 818–831. doi: 10.1016/j.ijproman.2010.07.002

Paquin, J.P., C. Gauthier, and P.P. Morin. 2016. "The Downside Risk of Project Portfolios: The Impact of Capital Investment Projects and the Value of Project Efficiency and Project Risk Management Programmes." *International Journal of Project Management* 34, no. 8, 1460–1470. doi: 10.1016/j.ijproman.2016.07.009

Pendharkar, P.C. 2014. "A Decision-Making Framework for Justifying a Portfolio of IT Projects." *International Journal of Project Management* 32, no. 4, 625–639. doi: 10.1016/j.ijproman.2013.09.006PMI Standard Committee. 2017. *The Standard for Program Management*, 4th ed. Newton Square, PMI.

Too, E.G., and P. Weaver. 2014. "The Management of Project Management: A Conceptual Framework for Project Governance." *International Journal of Project Management* 32, no. 8, 1382–1394. doi: 10.1016/j.ijproman.2013.07.006

Unger, B.N., H.G. Gemünden, and M. Aubry. 2012. "The Three Roles of a Project Portfolio Management Office: Their Impact on Portfolio Management Execution and Success." *International Journal of Project Management* 30, no. 5, 608–620. doi: 10.1016/j.ijproman.2012.01.015

CHAPTER 6

Project Systems for Strategic Transformation

- Traditional project management, complex project management, program management, and project portfolio management collectively serve to implement transformation driven by strategy.
- Implementation of organizational transformation relies on project management practices and on foundations of culture, structure, and capabilities resident in the organization.
- During the process of implementing strategic transformation, organizations need to consciously assess and continually enhance capabilities to pursue the best methods of implementation.

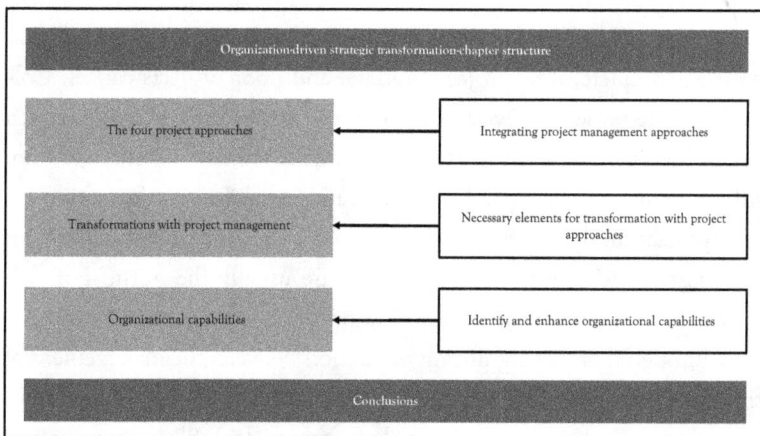

Chapter Structure

Integrating Project Management Techniques

The story so far indicates a separation of the four project management approaches: traditional project management, complex project management, program management, and project portfolio management. Indeed, each level of approach derives from the need to cover limitations. Traditional project management has a history of success for well-defined goals with few complexities. However, as projects became ever more complex, traditional approaches and methodologies proved inadequate. An early reaction was to adjust existing techniques and methodologies to accommodate complexity.

The approach to complex project management demonstrated effectiveness to a degree. Changes to the forms of control, interaction, and orientation stressed coverage of complexity due to structural additions and complications, the evolution of the environment over time, and new technology. However, directional complexity, that due to ambiguous goals and objectives, proved impossible to handle with simple adjustments. Program management emerged as the approach of choice for situations of directional complexity.

Program management remains flexible to changes with the express purpose of capitalizing on opportunities arising from a change in the environment or strategic direction of an organization. Program management achieves ambiguous goals through a collection of projects, each with its unique deliverable that moves the organization toward the goal of the program. Though each project in the program requires a clear definition, the collection of projects in the program is under constant flux as projects complete, new projects initiate, and poor projects cancel. Collectively, the projects move an organization in the desired direction even when the direction alters as the environment or strategies change. Even still, programs are insufficient in conducting a major transformation for an organization since even focused benefits do not typically transform an organization. Multiple benefits or goals are usually the norm. For that situation, the final approach of project portfolio management emerged.

Although there are significant differences between the management of traditional projects, complex projects, programs, and project portfolios, they all serve to realize organizational strategic goals. Table 6.1 summarizes the discussion to date. Project portfolio management progresses through

Table 6.1 Traditional projects, complex projects, programs, and project portfolios

Traditional Project Management	Motives	Project management enables the development of new services or products assuring: 1. Cost control 2. Quality assurance 3. Punctual delivery
	Elements	1. Temporary tasks implemented to create unique products, services, or results 2. Control of time, cost, scope, quality, risk, communication, resources, procurement, stakeholders
	Processes	Initiation-planning-directing-monitoring-closing
	Challenges	1. Uncertainty 2. Externalities
Complex Project Management	Motives	1. Clients may not understand their real needs as well as you think they do 2. Solutions for complex projects are numerous and vague
	Elements	1. For these projects, management is more difficult, and there are higher levels of uncertainty. Project goals are clear, but the solutions for achieving these goals are highly complex, with complexities stemming from structural complexity, technical complexity, and temporal complexity. 2. Interaction, Control, and Orientation
	Processes	First, identify which complexities are contained with the project, and then respond from the interaction, control, and orientation aspects.
	Challenges	1. Effective identification of project complexities 2. Selecting and adjusting tools for responding to project complexities 3. When uncertainty becomes ambiguity
Program Management	Motives	From uncertainty and ambiguity, we can obtain: 1. Opportunities to integrate strategy 2. Potential benefits and value generation
	Elements	1. Program management is for management of project combinations with high ambiguity, where we hope to create synergy through integration 2. Decision making-stakeholders-benefits
	Processes	Currently, there is no consistent management framework or standardized management technique for program management. However, the process of program management follows a specific life cycle: formulation-development-organizational-deployment-appraisal-dissolution

Countinue

	Challenges	1. Traditional project management concepts are firmly engrained 2. In program management, managers face new demands, for example, tolerance for ambiguity 3. Program goals are delimited
Project Portfolio Management	Motives	1. Selecting the best project portfolio under limited resources 2. The dilemma of project successes and strategic failures 3. Response to organizational strategy changes impacting multiple projects and programs
	Elements	1. Utilizing resources and organizational strategies to select and support multiple projects or investments. Project portfolio management progresses through project assessment, selection, and optimization of multiple project portfolios, ensuring that projects align with strategic goals and optimize organizational benefits 2. Interaction, Control, and Orientation
	Processes	1. Selection and analysis of project portfolio elements 2. Prioritization of project portfolio elements 3. Decision making of project portfolio plans 4. Project and program implementation and follow-up
	Challenges	1. The value of project portfolio elements is often difficult to judge

the selection of correct programs, complex projects, and traditional projects, prioritizing tasks, and providing organizational resources to achieve organizational strategy. Program management coordinates numerous projects and controls interconnected elements to achieve specific benefits. Complex project management is mainly concerned with finding solutions to work around uncertainties in projects stemming from structural complexities, technical complexities, and temporal complexities. Traditional projects are a process where plans are established and implemented within a given scope to serve the goals of an overall complex project, program, or project portfolio. Collectively, the ultimate purpose is the achievement of organizational strategic goals.

Leaving with the impression that each approach is independent of others would be erroneous; the approaches intertwine in an organization when effective. In fact, all approaches typically appear within an

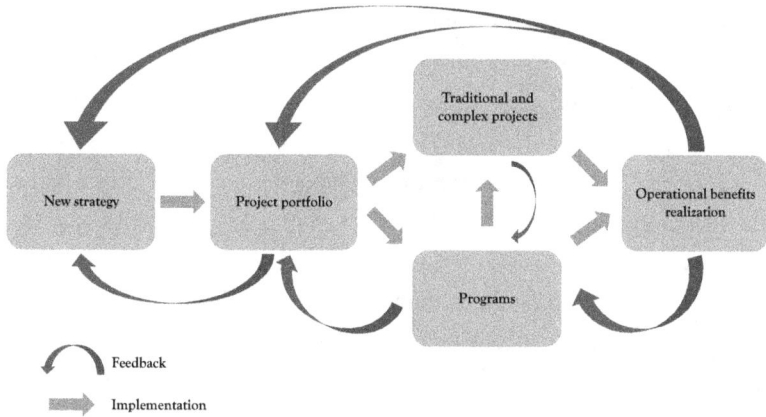

Figure 6.1 Transformation implementation and feedback paths

organization and perform as part of a complete system essential to the accomplishment of transforming the organization for strategic initiatives. Figure 6.1 illustrates the relationship among the approaches at a high-level, including strategic and operational endpoints. The straight arrows in the figure represent the path of implementation. As a new strategy is formulated, a portfolio will be created to secure the pursuit of the new strategy. Many possible programs and projects for achieving the strategy will be considered, but not all will be selected for portfolio inclusion. The output of the projects and programs implement as operations to achieve the desired benefits. Feedback occurs at multiple locations in the system, crossing the boundaries from one element of implementation to another. Feedback is for control purposes; to adjust ongoing portfolios, programs, or projects and also to provide material for improving organizational performance in future endeavors.

When executives formulate new strategies, the strategies develop arise partly from the internal and external environments of the organization. One aspect of the internal environment is the current operational practice and information about the benefits realized from those operations created by programs and projects. The performance of every project portfolio also feeds back to inform strategic development. Deeper into the system, each portfolio receives assessment information from the included projects, programs, and any operational benefits realized or failed to be realized. Programs spin off deliverables from multiple projects and receive information from operations about the performance of those deliverables to monitor progress toward the overall goals of the program. Programs must also coordinate all included projects, thus requiring feedback from those projects.

Though Figure 6.1 illustrates the implementation and feedback paths, even greater integration than the figure implies is required during the progress of transformation. Figure 6.2 deepens the explanation by illustrating the forward progress at the levels discussed throughout the book, though we omit the feedback loops of Figure 6.1 from Figure 6.2 to avoid clutter. Strategy formulation and planning begins at the highest level. Lower levels consider the hierarchy of project management approaches utilized in transformation. The figure shows the major phases in the life cycle for each approach. As strategies pass to project portfolio management, the cycle begins by identifying possible elements in the portfolio, analyzing the value of each possibility, and selecting those of highest value according to the resource constraints. The portfolio management team prioritizes the project and program elements to best meet the organizational strategy. The portfolio team plans the implementation in terms of resourcing and sequencing the programs and stand-alone projects. During implementation, the organization determines whether the presence of directional complexity requires a program management approach or a project management approach. Periodic assessment of the portfolio

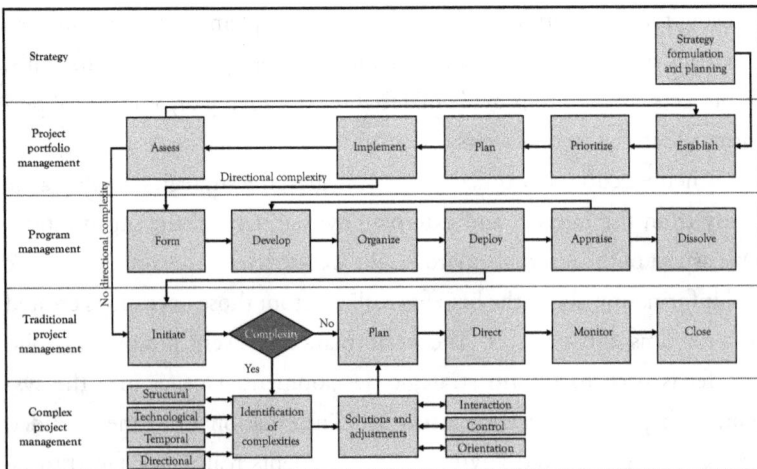

Figure 6.2 Integration of the four project categories

leads to the establishment of further programs and projects in the cyclical life cycle of portfolios, or indicates dissolution of the portfolio.

Upon selection of a program approach, a program management team assumes responsibility. Development of requirements and plans precedes organization, where program planning documents are then generated, and resources gathered. Deployment of the program launches multiple projects staged over time. The program team conducts frequent appraisals to evaluate the continued efficacy of each project and the possible addition of subsequent projects. Upon attainment of the program goals, the program terminates.

Upon the initiation of a project, the project team considers the level of complexity. If complexity is insignificant, the project continues with planning, directing, monitoring, and closing. Should complexity be significant; however, the project team must identify the complexities, choose appropriate solution techniques, or adjust current methodologies in interaction, control, and orientation to account for the complexities. Feedback occurs within and across all levels as indicated in the discussion earlier about Figure 6.1. Thus, though hierarchies exist, the implementation of any strategic transformation requires coordination of activities and resources across the approaches and levels, resulting in a system rather than a strict hierarchy.

How to Ensure the Success of Strategic Transformation

To this point, we built an understanding of the differences between the levels of project management approaches and considered an integrated execution structure. To effectively ensure that strategic organizational transformations are successfully implemented, we still need to consider essential foundations. In other words, we need to study how to connect project management principles with organizational structure, capabilities, and culture that support the implementation of the strategy (PMI Standards Committee 2017). Figure 6.3 shows the foundation of the organization in support of all project-related activities and operational activities. The implementation of operational activities, projects, complex projects, programs, and project portfolios achieves organizational strategic goals.

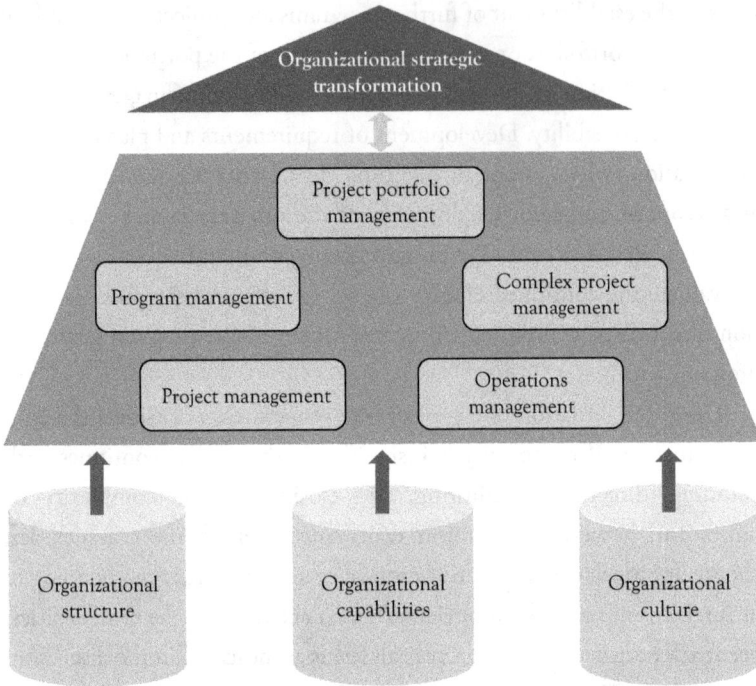

Figure 6.3 Organizational foundations for transformation efforts

The structural foundation supports an organization in the implementation of project portfolios, programs, and projects as well as operational activities. Often the amount of structure is determined by the nature of the organization. Many firms, especially in industries such as construction and technology, operate primarily in a project mode and build project managers into the authority hierarchy. Other companies often have a place for project managers in the organizational structure but are subordinate to functional managers under whom the projects typically reside. A form of matrix organization may be practical to allow projects or programs to reach across different functional areas, yet still retain a modicum of authority in the determination of resource allocation and personnel assignment. In addition to the project, program, and portfolio teams, an organization often builds permanent support structures for all project operations centered in a project management office, a program management office, or portfolio management office.

Organizational capabilities span a broad range. Not only must an organization have the ability to generate the products and services it offers to the market, but the organization must also have the talent for the management of traditional projects, complex projects, programs, and project portfolios. Continual learning from all operational and project experiences enhances talent at these levels, but also in a broader strategic capability. Not only is learning important in the creation and development of capabilities, learning is also critical to maintaining a current understanding of the environment that drives change requirements.

A common bromide in organizations is that people are resistant to change. However, an organization can develop a culture of change to counter resistance. The leadership team must be visibly supportive of all changes. The organization must provide adequate resources for the processes of transformation, thus transmitting a message of importance. Management at all levels should act to persuade others to accept and support any new direction. Communication must be prompt, inspirational, and focus on both the work effort required as well as the benefits expected. Rewards and work environments must reflect contributions to delivering transformation.

In summarizing the results of previous studies on strategic transformation, Franken et al. (2009) found similar advice to hold. Under strategic transformation, an organization must enhance its strategic transformation capabilities through effective management of three key processes:

1. Formulation and adjustment of project portfolio investments. Successful realization of strategic goals is achieved only through approval and optimization of wide-ranging programs, projects, and complex projects.
2. Implementation of strategic transformation. Effective adjustment and optimization of project portfolios can realize the expected benefits from the strategic transformation.
3. Enhancement of strategic transformation capabilities. Continued learning through strategic transformation techniques has proven effective and performance metrics proven informative is a way to enhance the transformation capabilities of an organization.

These three key points relate to the choice of portfolio elements, proper prioritization of the elements, and learning from implementation

Table 6.2 Ten key management elements of transformation implementation

Three key processes	Ten key management elements
Formulation and adjustment of project portfolios	1. Establish and strengthen a culture of continual change in organizations 2. Understand each transformation process in the early stages of its life cycle 3. Optimize plans relating to strategic goals to establish portfolios 4. Coordinate strategic leadership teams to support transformation portfolios
Implementation of strategic transformation	5. Establish detailed business cases to gather approval for transformation plans 6. Establish responsibilities and governance programs 7. Implement each transformation plan and realize the expected benefits 8. Manage ongoing transformation portfolios and solve issues relating to conflict, resources, and interconnectivity 9. Coordinate elements needed for transformational capabilities
Enhancement of strategic transformation capabilities	10. Review, learn, and enhance transformational capabilities

feedback. Further, Franken and colleagues found that the aforementioned three key points are broken down into "10 key management elements," shown in Table 6.2. Similarities exist with much of the discussion throughout this book or with common practices defined in standards for project, program, and portfolio management (IPMA; PMI Standards Committee 2017, 2018).

How to Enhance Strategic Transformation Implementation Capabilities

An organization facing constant challenges may find it difficult to internalize multiple experiences of project management and incorporate lessons from past strategic transformation implementations, which is a great loss for any organization. Therefore, from an organizational perspective, the question we need to ask is: how can we continually enhance our strategic transformational capabilities from a project management perspective?

The first step is to assess how well your organization realizes business benefits. Consider prior transformation initiatives for insight into which transformations you performed better versus those where your realization of benefits fell short. Take into consideration a complete analysis of impediments and facilitators along the dimensions of benefits, project approaches, organizational foundations, and strategies.

The second step is mainly concerned with presenting the assessment results to a strategic leadership team. The purpose of this is to convince the strategic leadership team of the necessity of enhancing strategic implementation capabilities. We recommend this discussion take place within a forum where the core purpose is to confirm the priority of potential business benefits and to obtain approval for funds and resources needed for developing greater capability or adjusting transformation plans.

The third step ties in with the key management practices of Table 6.2. Based on the results of the assessment in the first step and input from the second, consider performance in each of the 10 managerial elements listed. Determine the strong and weak managerial elements. If an organization becomes aware that its performance is lagging, it should not only terminate inadequate transformation plans but rapidly plug any capability lack critical to implementation, even before discussing alternate plans.

Finally, after determining which key factors require improvement, the final step is to determine the performance levels each factor can achieve. Achieving the results may require improvement to processes with the operation or project functions, greater integration of the different layers of project approaches, or improving the foundational elements.

In Conclusion

In this chapter, we integrated the different roles of traditional project management, complex project management, program management, and project portfolio management into a system perspective for an organization. We further provided an overview perspective on how to improve an organization's ability to conduct a strategic transformation. Throughout the earlier chapters, you were exposed to a high-level perspective of each element in the project management world. Specific tasks are not described or developed in this book; they are well established and documented in other publications. An excellent source for detailed material about processes and capabilities for the management of projects, programs, and project portfolios is the numerous publications of the Project Management Institute and the International Project Management Association. Many of these works appear in the reference list at the end of this chapter. Missing from these publications, however, is a perspective when to choose a particular approach, how they are integrated into an organization, and how an organization might develop the ability to apply these approaches to strategic transformation of an organization, all subjects introduced in this book.

Discussion Questions

1. Select your preferred strategic planning device or concept (e.g., strategy maps, balanced scorecard, and blue ocean). How would you use your choice to launch a portfolio?
2. What lines of communication must be in an organization to implement the system proposed in figures 6.1 and 6.2?
3. Describe an organizational culture receptive to implementing a full project management system. How would you construct such a culture in your organization?
4. Which foundation do you rate most high in the achievement of strategic transformation?
5. Describe the ripple effect of a failed project.

References

Franken, A., C. Edwards, and R. Lambert. 2009. "Executing Strategic Change: Understanding the Critical Management Elements that Lead to Success." *California Management Review* 51, no. 3, 49–73. doi: 10.2307/41166493

International Project Management Association. 2018. *Individual Competence Baseline for Portfolio Management*. Amsterdam, The Netherlands

International Project Management Association. 2018. *Individual Competence Baseline for Programme Management*. Amsterdam, The Netherlands

International Project Management Association. 2018. *Individual Competence Baseline for Project Management*. Amsterdam, The Netherlands

PMI Standard Committee. 2017. *PMBOK® Guide*. 6rd Edition. Newton Square, PMI.

PMI Standard Committee. 2017. *The Standard for Program Management*, 4th ed. Newton Square, PMI.

PMI Standard Committee. 2018. *The Standard for Organizational Project Management*. Newton Square, PMI.

About the Authors

Dr. James J. Jiang is Professor of Information Systems with National Taiwan University, Taipei, Taiwan. Dr. Jiang was the inaugural recipient of the Fu-Bon Endowed Professorship, National Taiwan University and the Dr. Yuan Tseh Lee Outstanding Chaired Professor of the Foundation for the Advancement of Outstanding Scholarship. Dr. Jiang served as a Distinguished Professor of information systems (IS), Australian National University, and a Research Professor of IS, University of Central Florida, for more than two decades. He was also the first recipient of the Business School Distinguished Scholar Award, University of New South Wales, Australia, in 2017. Prof. Jiang previously served as Senior Editor for *MIS Quarterly* and the *Journal of Association of Information Systems*. Currently, he is the Editor-in-Chief of the *Pacific Asia Journal of Association of Information Systems* and Departmental Editor of the *Journal of Management Science and Engineering* (JMSE) sponsored by the National Natural Sciences Foundation of China (NSFC). Professor Jiang's research interests center on information technology project, program, and portfolio management. He has over 200 academic journal articles on these and other topics and is internationally recognized as a top researcher in the IS and project management disciplines with a large number of highly cited articles.

Gary Klein is the Couger Professor of Information Systems at the University of Colorado, Colorado Springs. His research interests include project management, information system development, technology transfer, and mathematical modeling with over 200 academic publications in these areas. He is recognized as a top researcher in the field of information technology project and program management, with his papers garnering significant attention. Dr. Klein served as Director of Education for IPMA-USA and is an active member of both the Project Management Institute and the International Project Management Association. He is a Fellow of the Decision Sciences Institute where he leads the Specific Interest Group on Project Management. Dr. Klein held prior editorial posts with *MIS Quarterly*, the *Journal of the Association for Information Systems*, and *Comparative Technology Transfer and Society*. He currently serves as a Senior Editor for the *Pacific Asia Journal of the Association for Information Systems* and as an Editor-in-Chief of the *Project Management Journal*. Before pursuing an academic career, Dr. Klein consulted for information system deployment as part of a client-oriented firm and was Director of the IS department for a major financial institution.

Dr. Wei (Wayne) Huang is a Chaired Professor of Information Systems, and the Dean of Business of School, Southern University of Science and Technology, China. He also holds the Changjiang Chair Professor and the Directorship of the Collaborative Innovation Center of China Pilot Reform Exploration and Assessment, which is supported by the National Development and Reform Commission. The center aims to apply program management theoretical and professional knowledge and tools to aid the Chinese government's reform practices and resolve the challenges on how (local) governments can become more experimental, adaptive, and agile while at the same time delivering public and social value through digital government projects, programs, and portfolios. Before returning to China, Prof. Huang was a tenured Professor, Visiting Scholar, or Fellow at other top-tier research universities including the University of New South Wales, the University of Georgia, Ohio University, and Harvard University. He has authored or coauthored more than 60 academic articles in top international journals, such as the *Journal of Management Information Systems, Management Information Systems Quarterly, Decision Support Systems, the European Journal of Operational Research, OMEGA, IEEE & ACM Transactions,* and the *European Journal of Information Systems*. Prof. Huang is the Founding President of Association for Information Systems Special Interest Group on IS in the Asia Pacific. He served also as the Associate Editor for *Information & Management, the Asia Pacific Journal of Information Systems,* and as Editor-in-Chief of the *International Journal of Industrial Engineering & Management*.

Index

OTHER TITLES IN THE PORTFOLIO AND PROJECT MANAGEMENT COLLECTION

Timothy J. Kloppenborg, Xavier University, Editor

- *Agile Working and the Digital Workspace* by John Eary
- *Passion, Persistence, and Patience* by Alfonso Bucero
- *Adaptive Project Planning* by Louise Worsley and Christopher Worsley
- *The Lost Art of Planning Projects* by Louise Worsley and Christopher Worsley
- *Project Communication from Start to Finish* by Geraldine E. Hynes
- *Executing Global Projects* by James Marion

Announcing the Business Expert Press Digital Library

Concise e-books business students need for classroom and research

This book can also be purchased in an e-book collection by your library as

- a one-time purchase,
- that is owned forever,
- allows for simultaneous readers,
- has no restrictions on printing, and
- can be downloaded as PDFs from within the library community.

Our digital library collections are a great solution to beat the rising cost of textbooks. E-books can be loaded into their course management systems or onto students' e-book readers.
The **Business Expert Press** digital libraries are very affordable, with no obligation to buy in future years. For more information, please visit **www.businessexpertpress.com/librarians**. To set up a trial in the United States, please email **sales@businessexpertpress.com**.

www.ingramcontent.com/pod-product-compliance
Lightning Source LLC
Chambersburg PA
CBHW061326220326
41599CB00026B/5057